Gems from the Kitchen

Gems from the Kitchen

Maureen Dahl

KEY PORTER BOOKS

National Library of Canada Cataloguing in Publication Data

Dahl, Maureen
    Gems from the kitchen

Includes index.
Published in conjunction with the charity, Gems of Hope.
ISBN: 1-55263-411-6

1. Cookery. I. Gems of Hope (Association) II. Title.

TX714.D328 2002   641.5   C2002-900088-2

The publisher gratefully acknowledges the support of the Canada Council for the Arts and the Ontario Arts Council for its publishing program.

We acknowledge the financial support of the Government of Canada through the Book Publishing Industry Development Program (BPIDP) for our publishing activities.

Key Porter Books Limited
70 The Esplanade
Toronto, Ontario
Canada M5E 1R2

www.keyporter.com

Photographs appear by permission of Corning Canada Inc.

Design: Peter Maher
Photography: Pete Paterson
Electronic formatting: Heidy Lawrance Associates

Printed and bound in Canada

02 03 04 05 06 6 5 4 3 2 1

For the real "gems" of this organization—
our donors, volunteers and board members.
Without you, we would not be.

Contents

Introduction

Thank you for purchasing *Gems from the Kitchen*. In doing so, you've made an important contribution to an on-going effort to help women in developing countries help themselves. That's a vital part of the Gems of Hope mandate, and this cookbook is just one way that we can make our goal a reality. All proceeds from its sale will go directly to Gems of Hope and its projects.

For those of you who aren't familiar with our work, Gems of Hope is a small organization with a big vision—a vision that's focused on helping countless women improve quality of life for both themselves and their families. We work in some of the poorest communities in the developing world, focusing on women's health, education, and financial independence. Those involved with Gems of Hope believe strongly in this vision and are committed to achieving success.

Originally known as Global Education Medical Supplies (GEMS) Inc., Gems of Hope was founded in 1982 by Ben and Doreen Wicks. Their goal was to form an organization that would assist developing countries through the shipment of medical equipment and supplies. Following its inception, GEMS sent supplies—sometimes repeatedly—to Afghanistan, Angola, Argentina, Armenia, Bangladesh, Bolivia, Brazil, Colombia, Croatia, the Dominican Republic, Ecuador, Egypt, El Salvador, Ethiopia, Ghana, Grenada, Guatemala, Guyana, Haiti, Honduras, India, Iran, Jamaica, Jordan, Kenya, Lebanon, Liberia, Lithuania, Madagascar, Mozambique, Nicaragua, Nigeria, Panama, Pakistan, Peru, the Philippines, Romania, Sierra Leone, St. Kitts, St. Lucia, St. Vincent, Swaziland, Syria, Tanzania, Trinidad, Turkey, Uganda, the Ukraine, Vietnam, Zaire, and Zambia.

As the organization soon found out, though, the shipment of educational and medical supplies can be tricky. Delivery is expensive, and it's often difficult to determine if the materials are making it to those who need them most. Recognizing the need to develop a more effective approach to development assistance, GEMS began to shift some of its support to small-scale projects.

In 1987, for example, GEMS donated $50,000 to a Canadian nurse working in West Point, Liberia. With these funds, she was able to open a much-needed maternity clinic. Four years later, in 1991, GEMS helped get the Grassroots College project off the ground in Bennetland, Jamaica. The college taught the orphaned youth of AIDS victims reading, writing, mathematics, science, ethics, and behavior. It also offered job training in areas like shoemaking and repairs, cartography, bicycle repair, brick making, and agriculture. In 1992, the Grassroots College congratulated its first 19 graduates. Due to its success in Bennetland, the college has expanded to several other locations and is still going strong.

In 1996, GEMS took stock of its activities and once again redefined its mandate. The organization renamed itself Gems of Hope, and decided to concentrate on implementing micro-financing projects for women. It was a decision based on both need and desire. For Gems volunteers and supporters, the idea of working with the poorest of the poor was important—and it quickly became clear that this tended to mean women. Research suggested that in developing countries women were generally more disadvantaged than men. With training, however, they were often more successful in running small businesses. Most importantly, women tended to use the proceeds of their work for the feeding, clothing, and education of their children.

In order to successfully implement its projects and keep costs low, Gems of Hope establishes strong partnerships with local non-profit organizations. The goal is the creation of small-business loan programs. In communities where Gems is active, local women become part of a "village bank." Each woman can apply for a small-business loan of between $50 and $200. Along with their loans, these women receive primary health care training and basic education. They are taught math, basic bookkeeping, and how to open and administer bank accounts. As the individual businesses develop, the loans are repaid with interest. Remarkably, the default rate is almost non-existent—the village bank will help cover a client's payment if she is having a bad month. Since the bank as a whole is responsible for each individual loan, the women work together as a unit, attending weekly (or monthly) meetings. Between 1996 and 2000, Gems initiated micro-finance projects in Bangladesh, Bolivia, Brazil, Guatemala, India, Peru, the Philippines, and Vietnam.

Gems of Hope funding comes from independent donors, foundations, and the Canadian International Development Agency, as well as a series of annual events—including book sales, garden parties, barbecues, Salsa nights, golf tournaments, and the astonishingly successful Gems Festival of Hope, a gastronomic event held each year in Toronto. Featuring culinary treats provided by some of the best executive chefs in the city, the Festival attracts 600 guests each year and helps Gems raise in the range of $75,000.

Given the importance of food to our fundraising efforts—a garden party just isn't complete without tea and scones, and even book sales are more successful when homemade baked goods are also up for grabs—a cookbook seemed like a logical extension of our efforts. In the pages that follow, you'll find a host of tried-and-true recipes for all occasions. Many Gems' supporters and long-term volunteers have contributed their favorites—whether it's a mouthwatering dessert, a cool summer soup, or the shepherd's pie that's become a Sunday-night staple.

You'll find a number of recipes with an international flavor: from Guacamole, Chicken Adobo, and Thai Shrimp to Spicy Lentil Soup, Dal Curry, and Tandoori Chicken. I hope that, through preparing and enjoying these dishes, you'll develop an appreciation for the cultures and countries in which Gems does its work.

They are all good recipes for a good cause.

We hope you enjoy using this cookbook as much as we enjoyed putting it together. Bon appétit!

Maureen Dahl
2002

Appetizers and Snacks

Antipasto

If you like, increase the amount of your favorite ingredients, and remember to use a very good olive oil—extra virgin is best. You should have about 6 cups (1.5 L) of ingredients in bite-size pieces.

	Brussels sprouts, cooked crisp and cooled	
	Mushrooms (if large, cut in half)	
1	can artichoke hearts, drained and cut in half	1
	Hearts of palm	
	Black olives	
	Pickled hot peppers	
	Cherry tomatoes	
	Cheese cubes	
	Pepperoni cubes	

TIP: To cook brussels sprouts, peel off the dark outer leaves and cut a slice off the stem end. Cut an X in the end and drop the sprouts into boiling salted water. Cook for 4 to 5 minutes. Drain and immerse in cold water to stop the cooking process.

Dressing:

¹⁄₄ cup	red wine vinegar	50 mL
1 tsp	Dijon mustard	5 mL
³⁄₄ cup	olive oil	175 mL
¹⁄₂ tsp	granulated sugar	2 mL
	Salt and pepper	

DRESSING:

In small bowl, blend vinegar and Dijon, then whisk in olive oil. Add sugar and salt and pepper to taste; mix well. Makes 1 cup (250 mL) dressing.

In large bowl, pour dressing over sprouts, mushrooms, and artichoke hearts. One half hour before serving add hearts of palm and remaining ingredients; toss and arrange on platter or individual serving plates.

Makes 6 servings.

Braided Sausage Ring

This is a dish I take everywhere. It travels well, tastes delicious, is easy to make, looks beautiful, and is requested often. I usually serve it, sliced thickly, with Peach Chutney (page 102) or plum chutney.

1 lb	bulk sausage meat	500 g
1	medium onion, finely chopped	1
1-1/2 tsp	mixed herbs (try combination of sage, thyme, and rosemary)	7 mL
2 tbsp	chopped fresh parsley	25 mL
	Salt and pepper	
1	pkg frozen puff pastry	1
	Milk	

In bowl, combine sausage meat, onion, herbs, and salt and pepper to taste. Mix well, using your hands if you need to.

Roll out pastry to rectangle about 12 inches x 16 inches (22 x 40 cm) and lay sausage mixture down the long center. Make diagonal cuts into pastry on each side of sausage meat, about ½ inch (1 cm) apart. Dampen edges with milk and criss cross from each side over meat and tuck under. This will give braided effect. (You can use a little imagination with the design.) Brush with a little milk.

Bake in 425°F (220°C) oven for 20 minutes. Lower heat to 350°F (180°C) for about 25 minutes or until golden.

Makes about 12 slices.

Cheese Cookies

Linda Briggs works in computer sales. She makes these savory cookies for her friends. They are a particular hit at our cocktail parties.

1	tub MacLaren's Imperial Cheddar cheese	1
1/2 cup	margarine	125 mL
1 cup	all-purpose flour	250 mL
1/4 tsp	cayenne pepper (or more to taste)	1 mL
1-1/2 cups	crispy rice cereal	375 mL

In large bowl, mix cheese, margarine, flour, and cayenne. Fold in crispy rice cereal.

Roll mixture into small balls; place on cookie sheet and press with fork (dip fork in cold water first) to form cookies.

Bake in 350°F (180°C) oven for 12 to 15 minutes or until golden.

Makes 24 appetizer cookies.

Crab Hors d'oeuvres

This recipe came from a friend and long-time volunteer now living in Santa Barbara, California. Delicious and a breeze to make, you can keep a supply in the freezer for unexpected company.

½ cup	margarine	125 mL
4 oz	grated Cheddar cheese	100 g
1	can (7 oz/198 g) crab meat	1
4	green onions, chopped	4
Pinch	cayenne pepper	Pinch
5	English muffins	5
	Paprika	

In bowl, cream margarine and cheese. Add drained crab meat, chopped onions, and cayenne.

Split muffins in half, spread with crab mixture, and cut each half into 6 wedges. Freeze on a cookie sheet; store in plastic bags and use as needed. To use, broil until slightly brown and heated through. Sprinkle with paprika and serve warm.

Makes 60 appetizers.

Mini Crustless Quiches

These bite-size quiches are a big hit as finger food. You can use frozen spinach instead of fresh if you prefer.

1	pkg (10 oz/284 g) fresh spinach	1
1 cup	grated Cheddar cheese	250 mL
1 cup	grated mozzarella cheese	250 mL
1/2 cup	grated Parmesan cheese	125 mL
7	large eggs	7
1 tbsp	chopped fresh basil (or 1/2 tsp/2 mL dried)	15 mL
1/2 tsp	each salt and pepper	2 mL

TIP: You can substitute frozen spinach for the fresh. Use a 10 oz (284 g) package and follow the package directions for cooking and draining.

Cook spinach well, drain, and chop. Place in large bowl.

In separate bowl, combine three cheeses; reserve 1/2 cup (125 mL) of mixture for later.

Lightly beat eggs and add to spinach in bowl along with remaining ingredients. Mix well.

Pour into lightly greased 13- x 9-inch (3.5 L) baking dish. Bake at 350°F (180°C) oven for 15 minutes. Sprinkle with reserved cheese and return to oven for another 5 minutes.

Let stand for 15 to 20 minutes then cut into 1-1/2-inch (4 cm) squares.

Makes 54 squares.

Marg's Hot Crab Dip

Marg Munro-McCall sent this recipe to us. Very yummy! Marg is a "chef in training." She has her certificate in the fundamentals of French cooking and studied with famous French chefs at the Ann Whellan École du Cuisine Française in the Château du Fey, Burgundy, France. Marg loves to cook for her family and friends and enjoys a broad range of cuisine.

8 oz	cream cheese	250 g
½ cup	plain sour cream	125 mL
1	can (7 oz/198 g) crab meat, drained	1
2 tbsp	finely chopped parsley	25 mL
1 tsp	dry mustard	5 mL
2 to 3 dashes	Worcestershire sauce	2 to 3 dashes

Topping:

2 tsp	grated Parmesan cheese	10 mL
2 tsp	bread crumbs	10 mL

In large bowl, mix cream cheese and sour cream. Add crab meat, parsley, mustard, and Worcestershire; mix well. Place mixture in oven-proof serving dish and top with grated Parmesan cheese and bread crumbs. Bake in 350°F (180°C) oven for about 25 minutes or until hot and bubbly.

Serve with crackers or small breads.

Makes about 1-½ cups (375 mL).

Moe's Guacamole

I often serve this at our volunteer meetings, which seem to happen weekly. The gang gets together over a glass of wine to talk about kids, school, and future projects. This dish is very easy, healthy, and my friends can't seem to get enough of it.

3	ripe avocados	3
1	medium onion, chopped	1
3 to 4	chopped Roma tomatoes	3 to 4
1	clove garlic, finely minced or mashed (optional)	1
	Juice of 3 limes	
¼ cup	chopped fresh coriander (cilantro)	50 mL
	Seasoning salt	

Halve and pit avocados and scoop out flesh. In bowl, mash with fork.

Add chopped onion, tomatoes, garlic (if using), lime juice, coriander, and seasoning salt to taste. Guacamole will keep for up to two hours, covered with plastic, in refrigerator.

Makes about 3 cups (750 mL).

TIP: If you're not serving immediately, bury avocado pit in the mixture to prevent darkening, cover, and refrigerate. Enjoy! I like heat in most dishes, so I usually add two or three chopped fresh jalapeño peppers to this guacamole.

Olive Baguette Spread

This tasty appetizer spread is a favorite of Kathy Buchanan.

½ cup	oil	125 mL
1	large clove garlic, finely chopped	1
1	can (10 oz/284 mL) mushrooms, stems and pieces (drained and finely chopped)	1
3	pickled red peppers, finely chopped	3
½	jar (12 oz/341 mL) olives with pimientos, finely chopped	½
½ cup	tomato sauce	125 mL
1-½ cups	grated old Cheddar cheese	375 mL
	Pepper to taste	
1 to 2	baguettes	1 to 2

In large bowl, mix all ingredients except baguettes together and let stand for at least 3 hours in refrigerator.

Slice baguette into manageable pieces and place on cookie sheet. Spread olive mixture onto each slice and place in 300°F (150°C) oven for about 10 minutes or until heated through. Serve hot.

Makes 18 to 24 slices.

Potato Skins

Potatoes are like pizzas. You can put almost anything on them—but the traditional cheese and bacon on skins is still the most popular.

6	slices bacon	6
4	medium potatoes, baked	4
1-1/2 cups	shredded Cheddar cheese	375 mL
	Oil for deep frying	

Cook bacon; cool and crumble.

Cut potatoes in eighths. Scoop out pulp, leaving 1/4 inch (5 mm) of potato on skin.

Deep fry skins in hot oil for 1 to 2 minutes or until golden brown; drain on paper towels.

Sprinkle cheese onto skins and top with bacon; heat under broiler until cheese melts. Serve with sour cream.

Makes 32 appetizers.

Sweet and Sour Meatballs

TIP: To freeze the meatballs, follow directions for making meatballs, then set on a cookie sheet and place in freezer. When frozen, remove and place in freezer bag; return to freezer until ready to use. Meatballs can be added frozen to the prepared sauce. Just extend the simmering time by 10 minutes.

These easy-to-make meatballs can be prepared in advance and refrigerated or frozen, before cooking in the sauce. Double the recipe if you have a crowd.

15 oz	grape jelly	420 mL
12 oz	chili sauce	341 mL
1/2 tsp	lemon juice	2 mL
2 lb	lean ground beef	1 kg
2	eggs	2
1/3 cup	bread crumbs	75 mL
1 tbsp	chopped fresh parsley	15 mL
Pinch	nutmeg	Pinch
	Salt and pepper	

In deep saucepan, combine jelly, chili sauce, and lemon juice and bring to boil. Let simmer.

Meanwhile, in large bowl, mix ground beef with eggs, bread crumbs, parsley, nutmeg, and salt and pepper to taste. Roll mixture into bite-size balls and drop into sauce. Simmer, uncovered, for 30 minutes. Cover pan and cook for another 10 minutes or until meatballs are cooked through.

Makes about 24 meatballs.

Quick Layered Pesto Spread

This recipe comes from Maureen Cole, a dedicated Gems volunteer. Her beautiful smile and sense of humor have helped us through every major fundraiser during the past four years. (Try making your own Pesto Sauce; the recipe follows.)

8 oz	cream cheese, softened	225 g
1 cup	Pesto Sauce	250 mL
	(recipe follows)	
2	cloves garlic, minced	2
2	medium tomatoes, diced	2
	(plum tomatoes are best)	

Spread softened cream cheese over entire bottom of shallow serving platter or pie plate. Evenly spread pesto sauce over cream cheese. Sprinkle garlic over pesto and top with chopped tomatoes.

Place spreader or small spoon in dish and serve with toasted French bread.

Makes about 2-½ cups (625 mL).

TIP: You can serve your favorite crackers, toasted bagels or pita breads cut into wedges, or packaged cocktail rye bread.

Pesto Sauce

This aromatic basil and garlic sauce is terrific tossed with any type of pasta, spread over grilled fish, tomatoes, and many other foods. Use it in our Quick Layered Pesto Spread (page 23) appetizer.

4 cups	fresh basil	1 L
1/2 cup	pine nuts	125 mL
8	cloves garlic	8
2/3 cup	extra virgin olive oil	150 mL
1/2 cup	Parmesan cheese	125 mL
1 tsp	each salt and pepper	5 mL

In food processor, pulse basil, pine nuts, and garlic until finely chopped. Stir in oil, Parmesan cheese, salt, and pepper; mix on low speed just until blended.

Makes 2-1/2 cups (625 mL).

Meatballs in Vermouth

This is a Dutch dish from Catherine Mossop, who heads the Gems of Hope Fundraising Committee. Catherine got the recipe from her mother-in-law and says it's wonderful for entertaining: "We had many difficulties and challenges while going through the adoption process with our first child. This was fraught with fifteen months of emotional ups and downs that many of our friends lived through with us. Upon our return from China with our fabulous daughter, we had a big party for all our friends as a giant thank you for all their love and support. I didn't just double this recipe, I made five batches for 150 meatballs!"

TIP: **It's even better when prepared in advance (up to 2 days) and refrigerated or frozen (up to 1 month).**

1-1/2 lb	lean ground beef	750 g
1	egg, beaten	1
1	slice white bread, broken in small pieces	1
1 tbsp	ketchup	15 mL
1 tsp	salt	5 mL
1 tbsp	corn or canola oil	15 mL

In bowl, thoroughly combine ground beef, egg, bread, ketchup, and salt. Form mixture into about 30 small meatballs (about size of teaspoon). Roll balls between your palms to form well, so as not to fall apart while cooking.

Heat oil in nonstick or well-greased skillet. Add meatballs and brown completely. Remove and set aside while you make sauce. Reserve pan drippings.

Sauce:

2 tbsp	finely minced onion (or shallots)	25 mL
1	clove garlic, crushed	1
1/4 tsp	each salt and oregano	1 mL
2 tbsp	all-purpose flour	25 mL
1 tsp	dry mustard (do not use prepared mustard)	5 mL
1	can (10 oz/284 mL) beef bouillon	1
1 cup	water	250 mL
Dash	aromatic bitters	Dash
1/3 cup	rye whisky	75 mL
3 tbsp	sweet (red) vermouth	45 mL

TIP: **This dish can be served as a main course—wonderful with roasted garlic mashed potatoes and a green salad.**

Add onion, garlic, salt, and oregano to meatball pan drippings. Cook until onions are tender.

Blend in flour and mustard; cook until bubbly. Add bouillon, water, bitters, whisky, and vermouth. Cook, stirring constantly, until thickened. Add meatballs and simmer for 5 minutes.

Cool and refrigerate until serving; reheat.

Makes about 30 meatballs.

Soups

Black Bean and Sausage Soup

Make a double batch to feed a crowd. Everyone will love it.

	Oil	
½ cup	chopped celery	125 mL
½ cup	chopped onions	125 mL
½ cup	chopped carrots	125 mL
2	cloves garlic, finely minced	2
1 tbsp	chopped fresh basil	15 mL
½ tsp	dried thyme	2 mL
½ tsp	dried marjoram	2 mL
	Salt and pepper	
¼ cup	red wine	50 mL
4 cups	chicken stock	1 L
1	can (10 oz/284 mL) black beans	1
1 lb	cooked Italian sausage, sliced into	500 g
	½- to ¾-inch (1- to 2-cm) slices	

In large pot with some heated oil, sauté celery, onions, carrots, garlic, basil, thyme, marjoram, and salt and pepper to taste.

Add red wine; scraping bottom of pan, mix all together.

Simmer to reduce liquid in pan by two-thirds. Add chicken stock, beans, and sausage slices. Cook slowly for 15 to 20 minutes until vegetables are tender.

Makes 6 servings.

Garlic Soup

Glenna Crockford is another Gems tireless volunteer. Like most of our volunteers, she has a full-time career and a family to look after, but she still finds time to support many worthy causes (including her friends). Glenna said not to be worried about the amount of garlic used: "Don't be shy, once it's cooked, it's delicious."

1 tbsp	butter	15 mL
10	cloves garlic, minced	10
1 tbsp	all-purpose flour	15 mL
6 cups	beef stock	1.5 L
2 tbsp	chopped fresh parsley	25 mL
1/4 tsp	pepper	1 mL
	Salt	
4	eggs, beaten	4
6	slices French bread, toasted	6
1-1/4 cups	each shredded Swiss and mozzarella cheese	300 mL

In large heavy saucepan, melt butter over low heat. Add garlic and flour; cook, stirring frequently, for 3 to 5 minutes or until lightly browned.

Stir in stock, parsley, and pepper. Bring to boil over high heat, stirring constantly. Reduce heat to low; simmer, covered, for 20 minutes. Taste and add salt, if necessary. (Soup can be prepared ahead up to this point. Cool, cover, and refrigerate for up to 24 hours. Bring back to simmering point before proceeding.)

Slowly whisk eggs into soup. Heat gently, but do not boil or let soup get too hot or eggs will curdle.

Place 6 warm oven-proof soup bowls on baking sheet. Ladle soup into bowls. Lay slice of toast on each serving of soup. Sprinkle cheese evenly over toast. Place baking sheet under hot broiler and broil for 1 to 2 minutes or until cheese melts. Serve at once.

Makes 6 servings.

Chunky Gazpacho

You don't need a blender to make this chunky version of gazpacho. The croutons give it an interesting texture.

TIP: **Whirl this mixture in a food processor or blender to get a smooth gazpacho.**

3	large ripe tomatoes	3
1	large cucumber	1
1	small green pepper, diced	1
1	small onion, finely chopped	1
1	clove garlic, finely minced	1
2 cups	tomato juice	500 mL
3 tbsp	olive oil	45 mL
2 tbsp	lemon juice	25 mL
1 tbsp	Worcestershire sauce	15 mL
	Salt, pepper, and hot pepper sauce	
	Garlic croutons	

Peel, seed, and chop tomatoes and cucumber. Place in large bowl with green pepper, onion, and garlic. Combine tomato juice, oil, lemon juice, and Worcestershire sauce; pour over vegetables. Season to taste with salt, pepper, and hot pepper sauce. Chill. Garnish with garlic croutons.

Makes 6 servings.

Minestrone

This warm, hearty soup can be a meal in itself. Serve it with lots of crusty bread.

2	cans (each 28 oz/796 mL) tomatoes with herbs and spices, reserving liquid	2
	Chicken broth (to bring reserved liquid to 2-½ cups/625 mL)	
1	stalk celery, thinly sliced	1
1	large carrot, peeled and thinly sliced	1
2	cloves garlic, minced	2
1	large potato, peeled and diced into ½-inch (1-cm) pieces	1
½ cup	macaroni (shells or elbow), uncooked	125 mL
2 tsp	dried basil	10 mL
1 tbsp	dried parsley	15 mL
1	can (14 oz/398 mL) cut green beans, undrained	1
1	can (12 oz/340 ml) corn, undrained	1

Drain tomatoes, reserving liquid. Chop tomatoes and set aside.

Measure reserved liquid and add chicken broth to equal 2-½ cups (625 mL). Pour into large soup pot.

Add celery, carrot, garlic, potato, and macaroni; cover and bring to boil.

Reduce heat to simmer and cook for 20 to 25 minutes, stirring occasionally, until vegetables are tender. Stir in beans and corn and their liquids. Simmer for 2 minutes, then cover and let stand 5 minutes before serving.

Makes 6 servings.

Onion Soup

It's everyone's favorite. You can make a lighter version by using light cheeses. Don't be concerned if you don't have individual soup bowls. Just use an attractive casserole dish and serve the soup at the table.

1 tbsp	butter	15 mL
5 cups	thinly sliced sweet Spanish onions	1.25 L
2 tsp	minced fresh garlic	10 mL
1-1/2 tsp	granulated sugar	7 mL
1-1/2 tsp	all-purpose flour	7 mL
5 cups	beef stock	1.25 L
4	slices Dutch rusks or toasted French bread	4
1/2 cup	grated Cheddar cheese	125 mL
1/2 cup	grated mozzarella cheese	125 mL

In nonstick saucepan, melt butter and sauté onions and garlic until soft, about 5 minutes. Stir in sugar; cover and simmer over low heat for 20 minutes, stirring occasionally.

Stir in flour; add beef stock and bring to boil. Cover and simmer for 20 minutes.

Pour into 4 individual oven-proof soup bowls. Place 1 rusk on top of each soup bowl and sprinkle cheeses (mixed together) over top.

Place under broiler and broil just until cheese is melted. Serve immediately.

Makes 4 servings.

Salmon Chowder

TIP: If you prefer a thicker chowder, add a milk and flour mixture (2 parts milk to 1 part flour).

I've been making this for about twenty years. It's quick and delicious and one of my mom's favorites.

1	can (7 oz/175 g) red salmon, drained	1
½ cup	chopped onion	125 mL
2	medium new or red-skin potatoes, diced	2
1 cup	chicken stock	250 mL
1-½ cup	milk	375 mL
Dash	Worcestershire sauce	Dash
¾ cup	grated Cheddar cheese	175 mL
	Salt and pepper	
½ cup	frozen peas	125 mL

Drain salmon and break into pieces. Set aside.

In soup pot, sauté onions in some oil; add potatoes and continue to sauté for about 2 minutes.

Add chicken stock and simmer until potatoes are almost tender. Add milk and bring back to simmer. Add Worcestershire sauce, cheese, and salt and pepper to taste. When cheese has melted, add salmon and peas and continue to cook for about 2 minutes until heated through.

Makes 4 servings.

Opposite: Chunky Gazpacho (page 29)
Overleaf: Caesar Salad (page 37)

Spicy Lentil Soup

By a stroke of luck, Olinda Fernandas called our office to inquire about volunteering. That was about eighteen months ago. She has been a delightful inspiration in many ways and dedicated to helping women through international development, particularly in Goa.

3 tbsp	olive oil	45 mL
1	large onion, chopped	1
4	cloves garlic, sliced	4
1/2 tsp	cumin	2 mL
1/2 cup	green lentils	125 mL
1/2 cup	red lentils	125 mL
2	dried chilies, crushed	2
	(or 1/4 tsp/1 mL cayenne pepper)	
2	medium carrots, finely diced	2
2	stalks celery, finely diced	2
2	bay leaves	2
5 cups	vegetable stock (from bouillon cubes)	1.25 L
	Salt and pepper	
1 tbsp	rice wine vinegar (or juice of 1/2 lemon)	15 mL

In large saucepan, over medium heat, heat oil and sauté onions until golden; add garlic and cumin. Sauté for 2 to 3 minutes or until garlic is golden. Add remaining ingredients except vinegar (or lemon juice). Bring to boil, cover, and reduce heat to low. Let simmer for about 40 minutes or until vegetables are tender. Remove bay leaves.

Adjust seasoning to taste and add vinegar. Serve with crusty bread.

Makes 4 servings.

Overleaf: Pasta with Summer Vegetables (page 50)
Opposite: Chili con Carne (page 61)

Cream of Fresh Tomato Soup

TIP: You can use this process with almost any local sun-ripened vegetables, such as fresh green peas, asparagus tips, tiny brussels sprouts, little carrots, and so on.

This is terrific to make at the end of summer using vine-ripened tomatoes.

6 to 8	sun-ripened tomatoes	6 to 8
3 tbsp	butter (approx.)	45 mL
2	white onions, finely minced	2
2 cups	milk	500 mL
4 tsp	granulated sugar	20 mL
	Salt and pepper	
½ cup	heavy cream	125 mL
	Fresh minced parsley	

Place tomatoes in very hot (boiled) water for 2 minutes. Drain and peel tomatoes when cool enough to handle. Cut each tomato in half and remove seeds; chop and set aside.

In saucepan, melt 1 tbsp (15 mL) of butter and sauté onions until soft but not brown; add tomatoes and simmer for 15 minutes. Add milk, sugar, and salt and pepper to taste. Simmer for 10 minutes.

Prepare soup bowls with 1 tsp (5 mL) of butter and 2 tbsp (25 mL) of cream in each. Pour hot soup into bowls and garnish with minced parsley.

Makes 4 servings.

Salads

Asian Spinach Salad

Leanne Gibson has lent her wit and charm to our team of volunteers for the last couple of years. Leanne thinks it's best to prepare this dressing the day before serving.

1	bunch fresh spinach	1
1	red pepper, diced	1
3	stalks celery, chopped	3
1/2	red onion, thinly sliced	1/2
1 cup	cooked rice	250 mL
1-1/2 cups	unsalted cashews	375 mL

Dressing:

1/2 cup	extra virgin olive oil	125 mL
1/4 cup	soy sauce	50 mL
2	cloves garlic, crushed	2

DRESSING:

In small bowl, blend olive oil, soy sauce, and garlic.

Remove stems from spinach; wash, dry, and tear large leafs into bite-size pieces. In large salad bowl, combine spinach with remaining ingredients. Just before serving, toss with prepared salad dressing.

Makes 6 servings.

Broccoli Salad

Another salad from Leanne Gibson, this one is often the dish she carts to the family potlucks.

1	bunch broccoli,	1
	trimmed, peeled, and cut into bite-size florets	
1	red onion, diced	1
2/3 cup	raisins	150 mL
1/2 cup	sunflower seeds	125 mL

Dressing:

1 cup	mayonnaise	250 mL
1 tbsp	lemon juice	15 mL
1 tbsp	brown sugar	15 mL

DRESSING:

In small bowl, mix ingredients together, stirring well to combine.

In salad bowl, pour dressing over broccoli and toss well. Add onion, raisins, and sunflower seeds and toss well.

Makes about 6 servings.

Caesar Salad

Everyone in my family loves and knows how to make a Caesar salad, but this is the one I taught to my youngest son (now fifteen). Both my sons, Andrew and Daniel, have been volunteering with Gems for four years. Over the last year, Dan's fraternity brothers (Delta Upsilon) have worked our Festival of Hope and have held several fundraisers to support our programs.

Dressing:

2	egg yolks	2
3	medium garlic cloves	3
3	anchovy fillets	3
1/4 tsp	Worcestershire sauce	1 mL
Dash	hot pepper sauce	Dash
1 cup	olive oil	250 mL
2 tbsp	fresh lemon juice	25 mL
2 tbsp	white wine vinegar	25 mL
	Salt and pepper	
2	heads romaine lettuce	2
	Freshly grated Parmesan cheese	
	Croutons	

DRESSING:

In food processor, combine egg yolks, garlic, anchovies, Worcestershire, and hot pepper sauce. With motor running, gradually add olive oil. When mixture is thick, very slowly add lemon juice and vinegar. Season with salt and pepper to taste and refrigerate in glass jar until ready to use.

Wash and tear romaine lettuce into large bite-size pieces, discarding outer leaves.

To serve, toss romaine with dressing and top with freshly grated Parmesan cheese and croutons.

Makes 6 to 8 servings.

Tropical Chicken Salad

This salad makes the perfect summer lunch!

1	lemon	1
1	orange	1
1	golden delicious apple	1
1 cup	pineapple chunks	250 mL
3 cups	cubed cooked chicken	750 mL
½ cup	celery, thinly sliced	125 mL
1 cup	mayonnaise	250 mL
½ tsp	chopped fresh basil	2 mL
¼ cup	Grand Marnier	50 mL
⅓ cup	slivered almonds, toasted	75 mL

Wash lemon and orange. Remove zest with zester or small knife, being careful not to include pith. Chop zest very finely. Cut lemon and orange into sections and squeeze out juice; set aside.

Core and dice apple. In glass or stainless steel bowl, combine apple, pineapple, chicken, celery, and prepared fruit zest. Stir in juice mixture and refrigerate for at least 1 hour.

Mix mayonnaise, basil, and Grand Marnier; fold into chicken mixture. Sprinkle individual servings with toasted almonds.

Makes 4 main-dish servings.

Greek Salad

Linda Briggs makes this great party salad to serve about fifteen people. Cut the ingredients in half for a standard family salad.

3	tomatoes	3
2	cucumbers	2
3	green peppers	3
1	red onion	1
1/4	head romaine lettuce	1/4
12	black olives	12
1/2 lb	feta cheese, crumbled	250 g

Dressing:

1/2 cup	olive oil	125 mL
1/3 cup	vinegar	75 mL
1	clove garlic, smashed	1
2 tbsp	dillweed	25 mL
1 tbsp	granulated sugar	15 mL
1 tsp	oregano	5 mL
1/2 tsp	salt	2 mL
	Pepper	

Cut tomatoes, cucumbers, and peppers into large chunks. Cut onion in half and then into slices, so that you end up with half rings.

Break romaine lettuce into bite-size pieces.

In salad bowl, toss all ingredients together and then dress.

DRESSING:

In jar, combine olive oil, vinegar, garlic, dill, sugar, oregano, salt, and pepper to taste. Seal and shake to mix. Store any leftover dressing in refrigerator for another day.

Makes about 15 servings.

Marinated Vegetable Salad with Gorgonzola Dressing

I happen to be a "blue" lover. If you're not into the "blue cheese" family, leave it out and you can still enjoy this salad with the vinaigrette.

½ cup	sliced mushrooms	125 mL
1	small red onion, sliced thinly	1
1	head romaine, torn into pieces	1
2 cups	sliced zucchini	500 mL
½ cup	sliced radishes	125 mL

Marinade:

4 oz	crumbled gorgonzola cheese	115 g
½ cup	olive oil	125 mL
1 tbsp	each balsamic vinegar and lemon juice	15 mL
1	clove garlic, minced	1
½ tsp	each granulated sugar and salt	2 mL
Pinch	each pepper and paprika	Pinch

MARINADE:

In bowl, combine gorgonzola, olive oil, balsamic vinegar, lemon juice, garlic, sugar, salt, pepper, and paprika.

In large bowl, combine mushrooms and onion. Pour dressing over top and marinate overnight.

Just before serving, in large salad bowl, combine romaine, zucchini, and radishes. Add marinated vegetable mixture and toss.

Makes 4 to 6 servings.

Potato Salad

This salad in one of Debbie Farquhar's recipes and it's the best potato salad I've ever had. She says, "I'm always asked to bring this to BBQs and there is seldom anything left even though it's a party-size salad."

TIP: **This recipe is easily halved, if you wish. Use olives instead of dill pickles for a great variation.**

10	medium potatoes (Yukon Gold)	10
8	green onions, sliced	8
4	carrots, chopped into small pieces	4
3	ribs of celery, chopped	3
4	medium dill pickles, finely chopped	4
1 cup	light mayonnaise	250 mL
1/4 cup	pickle juice	50 mL
1/4 cup	Dijon mustard	50 mL
1/4 cup	chopped fresh parsley	50 mL
1/8 cup	chopped fresh dill	25 mL
8	hard-cooked eggs (optional)	8
	Sprigs of fresh parsley or dill for garnish	

Boil whole potatoes until just tender (try not to overcook). Drain and rinse in cold water; set aside to cool.

In large bowl, assemble other ingredients except eggs and garnish. Cut potatoes into bite-size pieces, add to bowl, and combine well. If using eggs, quarter and chop; fold into salad. Garnish with parsley or dill and serve.

Makes 10 servings.

Spinach Salad

This lovely version of spinach salad was submitted by Kathy Buchanan.

| 1 | bunch fresh spinach | 1 |
| 1 pint | strawberries | 500 g |

Dressing:

½ cup	vegetable oil	125 mL
⅓ cup	granulated sugar	75 mL
¼ cup	white vinegar	50 mL
2 tbsp	each sesame and poppy seeds	25 mL
4 tsp	minced onion	20 mL
½ tsp	Worcestershire sauce	2 mL
¼ tsp	paprika	1 mL

Remove stems from spinach; wash and pat (or spin) dry.

Wash and slice strawberries. In large bowl, toss with spinach.

DRESSING:

Combine oil, sugar, vinegar, sesame and poppy seeds, onion, Worcestershire, and paprika. Toss with spinach and strawberries to coat well.

Makes 6 servings.

Springtime Salad

There's such a delicious variety of greens out there these days. Experiment with something a little different once in a while.

8 cups	assorted greens	2 L
½ cup	feta cheese (crumbled)	125 mL
1	can (4 oz/113 g) mandarin oranges (drained)	1
½ cup	fresh cranberries	125 mL
1	small red onion, chopped	1
½ cup	toasted pecans	125 mL

Dressing:

½ cup	canola oil	125 mL
¼ cup	red wine vinegar	50 mL
¼ cup	granulated sugar	50 mL
½ tsp	hot pepper sauce	2 mL
½ tsp	salt	2 mL
¼ tsp	black pepper	1 mL

DRESSING:

In bowl, whisk canola oil, vinegar, sugar, hot pepper sauce, salt, and pepper.

In large salad bowl, combine all other ingredients. Pour dressing over salad just before serving.

Makes 6 servings.

Meatless Main Courses

Black Bean and Corn Chili

This is a terrific low-fat, high fiber meal!

	vegetable oil	
2	medium-size onions, chopped	2
2	cloves garlic, minced	2
1/4 to 1/2 cup	canned jalapeños (or 3 to 6 fresh)	50 to 125 mL
2 tsp	dried oregano	10 mL
1-1/2 tsp	dried cumin	7 mL
1/4 tsp	black pepper	1 mL
1 cup	diced canned tomatoes with liquid	250 mL
1 cup	beer	250 mL
2 tbsp	tomato sauce	25 mL
2	cans (each 19 oz/540 mL) black beans, rinsed	2
2	cans (each 12 oz/341 mL) corn niblets	2

In large skillet, heat some vegetable oil and cook onions until translucent; add garlic, jalapeños, oregano, cumin, and pepper and stir-fry for 1 minute.

Add tomatoes and liquid, beer, and tomato sauce; simmer for about 10 minutes. Add beans and corn and simmer for 1 hour.

Makes 6 to 8 servings.

Cottage Cheese-Stuffed Peppers

This recipe comes from a dear old friend and volunteer, who wishes to remain anonymous. She is a wonderful cook and specializes in "country cooking."

3	large peppers, halved and seeded	3
3 tbsp	chopped onion	45 mL
3 tbsp	butter or margarine, melted	45 mL
2 cups	cooked rice	500 mL
1/2 tsp	Worcestershire sauce	2 mL
1/4 tsp	dried thyme	1 mL
1/4 tsp	salt	1 mL
1-1/2 cups	creamed cottage cheese	375 mL
1 cup	tomato sauce	250 mL

In pot of boiling salted water, partially cook peppers for 5 minutes; drain well.

In skillet, heat 2 tbsp (25 mL) butter and slowly cook onion, stirring occasionally, until lightly browned. In large bowl, pour cooked onion over rice; add Worcestershire, thyme, and salt; mix well. Stir in cottage cheese and tomato sauce; spoon mixture into pepper shells and brush filling with remaining butter. Bake in 375°F (190°C) oven for 30 minutes or until tender.

Makes 6 servings.

Creamy Mushroom, Broccoli, and Rice Bake

Here's another delicious item from my dear old friend.

2 tbsp	butter or margarine	25 mL
½ cup	chopped onions	125 mL
2-½ cups	cooked rice	625 mL
1	can (10 oz/284 mL) cream of mushroom soup	1
1	pkg (10 oz/284 g) frozen chopped broccoli, thawed	1
½ cup	grated Cheddar cheese	125 mL

In saucepan, melt butter; cook onions just until softened. Stir in rice, soup, and broccoli.

Transfer mixture to buttered shallow 6-cup (1.5 L) casserole or baking dish and top with cheese. Bake in 350°F (180°C) oven for 30 minutes or until heated through.

Makes 6 servings.

Dal Curry

This Indian dish was submitted by Olinda Fernandes. Serve the curry with rice.

1-1/2 cups	Masoor Dal (orange lentils)	375 mL
3 cups	water	750 mL
3	medium tomatoes, chopped	3
1 cup	chopped fresh coriander	250 mL
1	medium onion, finely sliced	1
3	cloves garlic, finely chopped	3
1/2 tsp	mustard seed	2 mL
1/4 tsp	dried cumin	1 mL
1/4 inch	fresh gingerroot, finely chopped (or grated)	5 mm
4	fresh or dried curry leaves	4
	(found in Asian grocery stores)	
	Salt	

Pick over lentils and rinse. In large saucepan, bring water to boil, add lentils, and simmer for 15 minutes. Add tomatoes and simmer for 5 minutes; add coriander and remove saucepan from stove.

In skillet, fry onions until brown; add garlic, mustard seed, cumin, ginger, curry leaves, and salt to taste. Cook, stirring, for about 2 minutes.

Stir onion mixture into lentils.

Makes 6 servings.

Egg and Potato Cake

TIP: **Egg and Potato Cake is finished under the broiler, so make sure to use a pan with a removable or heat-resistant handle.**

This dish is like an Italian frittata—*a heartier version of an omelette.*

2 tbsp	butter	25 mL
1	medium onion, diced	1
1-1/4 cups	peeled diced raw potatoes	300 mL
6	eggs	6
3 tbsp	water	45 mL
2 tbsp	chopped fresh parsley	25 mL
3/4 tsp	seasoned salt	4 mL
Pinch	dried thyme	Pinch

In 9-inch (23-cm) frying or omelette pan, melt butter. Add onion and potatoes; sauté for about 10 minutes or until potatoes are tender.

In bowl, beat eggs; add water, parsley, salt, and thyme and beat until blended but not frothy; pour over onion and potato mixture in pan.

Cook slowly; as eggs set, lift with spatula to allow uncooked portions to run underneath. When eggs are almost set on top, place pan under broiler 6 inches (15 cm) from heat for 1 to 2 minutes.

Turn out, without folding, onto heated serving platter.

Makes 4 servings.

Fettuccine Alfredo

Here's a great traditional pasta, whether it's served as a main course with a salad or as a side dish.

1 lb	fresh fettuccine	500 g
1 cup	freshly grated Parmesan cheese	250 mL
1 cup	whipping cream	250 mL
	Bacon bits (optional)	

In large saucepan of boiling water, cook fettucine until *al dente* (tender but firm); drain and return to saucepan.

Add Parmesan and cream; mix over medium heat, stirring constantly, for 3 minutes.

Place on serving plate and serve sprinkled with bacon bits (if using).

Makes 4 servings.

TIP: When using Parmesan cheese, particularly in an Alfredo sauce, try to use the best quality. Buy Parmigiano Reggiano and grate it, as you need it.

TIP: A good quality pasta will hold its *al dente* state for a while even if you overcook it by a minute or two, while inferior pasta will go limp soon after it is drained.

Pasta with Summer Vegetables

TIP: **Try using diced eggplant, yellow squash, and zucchini and a thinly sliced fennel bulb instead of the mushrooms, asparagus, and peas.**

You can substitute fusilli or penne for the pasta bow ties.

1 lb	pasta bow ties	500 g
2 tbsp	extra virgin olive oil	25 mL
2	garlic cloves, minced	2
1	medium red onion, peeled and thinly sliced	1
½ lb	mushrooms, thinly sliced	250 g
½ lb	asparagus, cut in 1-inch (2.5-cm) pieces	250 g
1	each red and green pepper, seeded and cut into 1-inch (2.5-cm) strips	1
2	sprigs fresh rosemary (or 1 tsp/5 mL dried)	2
½ lb	sugar snap peas	250 g
1 tbsp	orange zest	15 mL
1 tsp	dried thyme	5 mL
¼ cup	dry white wine	50 mL
¼ tsp	salt	1 mL
½ tsp	pepper	2 mL
3 tbsp	balsamic vinegar	45 mL
	Rosemary or dill sprigs	

In large pot of boiling salted water cook pasta according to package directions or until *al dente* (tender but firm). Drain and keep warm.

Meanwhile, in large skillet over high heat, heat olive oil. Add garlic and onion and cook, stirring, for about 2 minutes. Add mushrooms, asparagus, red and green peppers, and rosemary. Cook, stirring, for 3 minutes. Add peas, orange zest, thyme, and wine. Reduce heat to medium and cook for 5 minutes, or until vegetables are tender crisp.

Remove from heat; remove rosemary stems and add salt, pepper, and vinegar. Toss with pasta and serve hot or at room temperature. Garnish with sprigs of fresh rosemary or dill.

Makes 4 to 6 servings.

Macaroni Vegetable Medley with Wine

This hearty meatless casserole makes a terrific one-dish family supper.

Prepare, and set aside:

2 cups	elbow macaroni	500 mL
1	pkg (10 oz/284 g) frozen mixed vegetables	1
2 tbsp	butter or margarine	25 mL
3 oz	chopped fresh mushrooms	75 g
1/2 cup	chopped onion	125 mL
1	can (10 oz/284 mL) cream of celery soup (condensed)	1
1 cup	milk	250 mL
2 tsp	Worcestershire sauce	10 mL
1 tsp	each salt and white pepper	5 mL
1/4 tsp	dry mustard	1 mL
1/2 cup	dry sherry (or white wine)	125 mL
1/4 cup	chopped pimiento	50 mL
1 cup	cooked peas	250 mL
1/2 lb	Swiss cheese, grated	250 g

In separate pots, cook macaroni and frozen vegetables, following package directions; drain and set aside.

In skillet, melt butter; stir in mushrooms and onion. Cook, stirring occasionally, until onion is soft.

In large bowl, mix soup, milk, Worcestershire sauce, salt, pepper, mustard, and sherry. Add pimiento, peas, Swiss cheese, mushroom mixture, mixed vegetables, and cooked macaroni. Mix well and turn into buttered casserole dish. Bake in 300°F (150°C) oven for about 30 minutes or until thoroughly heated.

Makes 6 servings.

Meatless Lasagna

A lasagna dish doesn't need to have meat in it to be rich and satisfying.

2-¹/₂ cups	tomato sauce	625 mL
¹/₂ lb	lasagna noodles, cooked	250 g
¹/₂ lb	sliced processed cheese, cut in thirds	250 g
2 cups	creamed cottage cheese	500 mL
¹/₂ cup	grated Parmesan cheese	125 mL

To assemble lasagna: Spread ¹/₂ cup (125 mL) of tomato sauce in bottom of rectangular 8-cup (2-L) baking dish. Top with layer of ¹/₄ of the noodles, ¹/₃ of the cheese slices, separated, and ²/₃ cup (175 mL) of cottage cheese spooned evenly over top. Sprinkle with some Parmesan cheese and spread another ¹/₂ cup (125 mL) tomato sauce over. Repeat layers two more times. Top with layer of noodles, remaining tomato sauce, and Parmesan cheese.

Bake in 350°F (180°C) oven for 35 minutes.

Makes 6 servings.

Potato and Cauliflower Curry

Olinda Fernandes, one of the world's free spirits, sent this recipe. Olinda was raised in Kenya and now lives with her family in Toronto. She is a great supporter of international development and a dedicated volunteer.

¼ cup	vegetable oil	50 mL
1 tsp	crushed red chilies (add more to taste)	5 mL
½ tsp	dried cumin	2 mL
2	medium onions, sliced	2
2	cloves garlic, finely chopped	2
1 tsp	finely chopped ginger	5 mL
1 tsp	chili powder (or cayenne)	5 mL
1 tsp	salt	5 mL
Pinch	turmeric	Pinch
3	medium potatoes, cubed	3
½	head cauliflower, cut in florets	½
⅔ cup	water	150 mL
¼ cup	fresh coriander	50 mL

In large saucepan, heat oil. Add crushed chilies and cumin and stir. Add onions and sauté over medium-high heat until golden.

In small bowl, mix together garlic, ginger, chili powder, salt, and turmeric; add to onions and cook, stirring, for 2 minutes.

Add potatoes and cauliflower; stir to coat vegetables with spice mixture. Reduce heat to medium; add water and coriander. Simmer, covered, for 20 minutes or until potatoes are tender.

Makes 4 servings.

Meat and Poultry

Standing Rib Roast of Beef

TIP: Have your butcher loosen back, chine, and bone by sawing across ribs; then have the roast tied. This will make carving easier.

Company coming? You can never go wrong with a traditional roast of beef. Serve with Yorkshire Pudding (page 109) and horseradish.

3 to 4	rib, standing rib roast of beef	3 to 4
	Salt and pepper to taste	

Place roast in roasting pan, fat side up and season with salt and pepper to taste. If using a meat thermometer, insert in center of thickest lean part. Be sure thermometer bulb does not rest on bone or in fat.

Roast at 325°F (160°C). Allow 23 to 25 minutes per pound (500 g) for rare; 27 to 30 minutes per pound (500 g) for medium; and 32 to 35 minutes per pound (500 g) for well done. If using thermometer, roast is done when temperature registers 140°F (60°C) for rare; 150°F (65°C) for medium; and 170°F (75°C) for well done.

Let roast rest in warm place for 10 to 15 minutes. This will allow juices to settle and carving will be easier.

Beef and Pasta Bake

This dish comes under the heading of "comfort food" and is loved by kids of all ages. Serve it with crusty bread.

2 tbsp	olive oil	25 mL
1 lb	lean ground beef	500 g
3	cloves garlic, minced	3
3/4 cup	prepared spaghetti sauce	175 mL
3/4 cup	prepared brown gravy	175 mL
1/2 cup	milk or light cream	125 mL
1/4 cup	grated Parmesan or Romano cheese	50 mL
1 tsp	dried oregano (whole, not ground)	5 mL
1/2 tsp	dried rosemary (whole, not ground)	2 mL
	Salt and pepper	
3/4 lb	penne pasta	375 g
1-1/2 cups	grated mozzarella cheese	375 mL

In large frying pan, heat oil and add beef and garlic. Sauté until meat is tender; drain excess fat.

Add spaghetti sauce, gravy, milk, Parmesan cheese, oregano, rosemary, and salt and pepper to taste. Let simmer.

Meanwhile, in large pot of boiling water, cook pasta until just barely tender; drain and mix with meat sauce.

Pour into 13- x 9-inch (3.5 L) baking dish; top with mozzarella and bake in 350°F (180°C) oven for 25 minutes or until bubbly.

Makes 6 servings.

Shepherd's Pie

Here's a bit of trivia: Shepherd's Pie was originally made with lamb. A similar dish, like the version below, made with ground beef, was called Cottage Pie.

2 tbsp	vegetable oil	25 mL
1	medium onion, chopped	1
1	large carrot, chopped	1
1-½ lb	lean ground beef	750 g
	Salt and pepper	
4	large baking potatoes	4
¼ cup	milk	50 mL
¼ cup	butter	50 mL
1	can (10 oz/284 mL) creamed corn	1

In large skillet, heat oil and sauté chopped onion and carrot until lightly browned; remove from pan with slotted spoon.

Add ground beef to pan and cook until brown. Drain any excess fat; add onion, carrot, and salt and pepper to taste. Set aside.

Boil potatoes until tender; drain and mash well. Add milk, butter, and salt to taste and stir with fork until incorporated.

Place beef mixture in bottom of 2-quart (2.5-L) casserole dish. Spread creamed corn over mixture and top with mashed potatoes. Bake in 375°F (190°C) oven for 20 to 25 minutes or until top is light brown.

Makes 6 to 8 servings.

Steak with Herb-Spice Rub

Serve these steaks with grilled vegetables and a garden-fresh salad for a summer meal. You can broil the steaks instead of grilling, if you prefer.

2	cloves garlic, pushed through press	2
1 tbsp	chili powder	15 mL
2 tsp	dried oregano	10 mL
1-1/2 tsp	each ground cumin, dry mustard, salt, and pepper	7 mL
1/2 tsp	cayenne pepper	2 mL
4	bone-in rib-eye steaks (each about 10 oz/285 g)	4

In small bowl, mix garlic, chili powder, oregano, cumin, mustard, salt, pepper, and cayenne. Rub mixture onto both sides of steaks and let sit for 10 minutes.

Brush grill with oil. Grill steaks over medium heat for 4 to 5 minutes per side for medium doneness.

Makes 4 servings.

Tam Tam

This recipe comes from Anna, a great warm-hearted gal from Wisconsin. Tam Tam is a "good old-fashioned" comfort food, perfect on a cold winter night. And, like a lot of these dishes, it gets better with age. Reheat it for lunch the next day.

4	strips bacon, chopped	4
1	large onion, chopped	1
4 lb	ground beef	2 kg
2	cans (each 28 oz/796 mL) whole tomatoes, chopped	2
1	can (10 oz/284 mL) tomato soup	1
2 tbsp	granulated sugar	25 mL
2 tbsp	Worcestershire sauce	25 mL
2 tsp	salt	10 mL
1 tsp	pepper	5 mL
3	cans (each 19 oz/540 mL) red kidney beans	3

In skillet, sauté bacon. Add onion and cook until golden brown.

In another deep pan, brown ground beef; drain, and add bacon and onion mixture that has not been drained. Add tomatoes, soup, sugar, Worcestershire sauce, salt, and pepper. Simmer at least 1 hour.

Add kidney beans and cook for another 30 minutes. Serve with hot buttered bread as you would chili.

Makes 10 to 12 servings.

Beef Bourguignon

Mary Moylum, a busy Ottawa professional who recently published her first novel, The Snakeheads, *sent us this recipe. She says, "My favorite one-pot meal for busy, cold, blustery days is Beef Bourguignon."*

3	slices bacon (optional)	3
2 lb	round sirloin, cut in 2-inch (5-cm) cubes	1 kg
2 tbsp	all-purpose flour	25 mL
2	large potatoes, diced	2
1/2 cup	red wine	125 mL
2 cups	water (or beef broth)	500 mL
1	large onion, sliced	1
1/2 lb	mushrooms, sliced	250 g
1	rib celery, chopped	1
2	carrots, peeled and diced	2
2 tbsp	tomato paste	25 mL
	tofu (optional)	

In Dutch oven, brown bacon then discard, retaining bacon fat (use 2 tbsp/25 mL oil if not using bacon). In plastic bag, toss beef with flour; sear in bacon fat (or oil) until brown. Cook meat in batches.

Return beef to Dutch oven; add potatoes, wine, and water. Bring to boil; reduce heat to low and cook, covered, for 2 hours or until meat is tender.

Meanwhile, in skillet, fry onions and mushrooms and set aside. In separate pan, cook celery, carrots, and tomato paste for 5 minutes. Add to mushrooms and onions.

When meat is tender, add cooked vegetables to Dutch oven and simmer for another 30 minutes. (This is where you add the tofu if using.)

Makes 6 to 8 servings.

TIP: **This is a good recipe to hide a large block of tofu (about 8 oz/250 g). But add it in the last 20 minutes of the cooking process or it breaks down into very small pieces. On the other hand, it's a good way to get the family to consume it.**

TIP: **When entertaining, spruce up the meal by serving the Beef Bourguignon with wild rice.**

Beef Brochettes

Debbie Farquhar is a long-time Gems volunteer and she enthusiastically tested recipes submitted for this book. This is one of Debbie's own fabulous entrées.

1-1/2 to 2 lb	beef sirloin, in 1- to 1-1/2-inch (2.5- to 4-cm) cubes	750 g to 1 kg
8	large mushrooms	8
8	large cherry tomatoes	8
8	pieces green pepper	8
2	small onions, quartered	2
	Marinade (recipe follows)	

Place beef in prepared marinade for 2 hours, or preferably refrigerate overnight in freezer bag.

Use either metal or wooden skewers (if using wooden, soak in water for 30 minutes to prevent burning).

Divide beef into 8 servings. Skewer beef, alternating with mushroom, cherry tomato, piece of pepper, and onion quarter on each skewer.

Place finished brochettes on lightly oiled, preheated grill. Grill over medium-high heat for 10 to 15 minutes. Turn as each side is cooked and baste with marinade during process.

Makes 4 servings.

Marinade:

1/4 cup	olive oil	50 mL
2	large cloves garlic, minced	2
	Juice of one lime	
2 tbsp	soy sauce	25 mL
1 tbsp	brown sugar	15 mL
1 tsp	chili paste (or 1/2 tsp/2 mL chili flakes)	5 mL

In bowl, mix together all ingredients and use as directed for Beef Brochettes.

Chili con Carne

This recipe comes from a friend in Hot Springs, Virginia. It makes a lot of chili, but it freezes well and is even better reheated.

1 lb	hot or sweet Italian sausages	500 g
2 tbsp	vegetable oil	25 mL
2	onions, chopped	2
4	cloves garlic, crushed	4
2 lb	lean ground beef	1 kg
2	cans (each 19 oz/540 mL) Italian tomatoes, crushed	2
1	can (4 oz/113 g) green chilis	1
2 tbsp	Worcestershire sauce	25 mL
2 tbsp	hot pepper sauce	25 mL
1 tbsp	tomato paste	15 mL
2 tbsp	chili powder	25 mL
1 tbsp	salt	15 mL
1 tsp	each pepper and oregano	5 mL
1 tbsp	each celery salt, coriander seeds, coriander leaves, and cumin	15 mL
1 tsp	crushed red pepper flakes	5 mL
2	cans (each 19 oz/540 mL) red kidney beans	2

Slice sausages into 1-inch (2.5-cm) pieces. Place in large stockpot or Dutch oven with a little oil. Sauté until well browned. Remove to mixing bowl and drain fat from Dutch oven. Add remaining oil and gently cook onions until soft. Add garlic and beef. Sauté quickly.

Stir in remaining ingredients (including sausage) except kidney beans. Cover and cook over low heat for 2 hours, stirring occasionally. Stir in kidney beans and cook for 1 hour.

Makes 10 to 12 servings.

Grilled Leg of Lamb

TIP: When a leg of lamb has been boned, you can lay it out flat. This is called "butterflied." You will see the varying thickness of the meat. When grilled, the thick pieces will be rarer than the thin ones. This gives you a variety of doneness to offer your guests.

TIP: A 5 to 6 lb (2.5 to 3 kg) leg of lamb boned and trimmed will give you 3-1/2 to 4-1/4 lb (1.75 to 2.25 kg) of meat.

In most large supermarkets, you can buy frozen boneless butterflied New Zealand spring lamb legs. Better still, have your butcher bone and butterfly a fresh leg of lamb for you. Mint sauce or mint jelly is a wonderful accent.

2 cups	red wine	500 mL
1 tsp	each garlic powder, oregano, and rosemary	5 mL
1/2 tsp	dried thyme	2 mL
1	bay leaf	1
1	leg of lamb (4 lb/2 kg), boneless	1

In bowl, mix red wine and seasonings together. Marinate lamb flat for 6 to 8 hours or overnight in refrigerator.

Grill lamb over medium-high heat for about 20 to 30 minutes on each side or until desired doneness. Baste with marinade, if desired. Slice and serve.

Makes 6 to 8 servings.

Lamb Chops with Pasta and Garlic Hollandaise

¼ lb	spinach linguine	125 g
¼ lb	tomato linguine	125 g
2 to 3	cloves garlic, peeled	2 to 3
	Olive oil	
1 cup	Hollandaise Sauce	250 mL
	(recipe, page 72)	
12	lamb loin chops	12
	Chopped fresh parsley	

In large pot of boiling water, cook pasta until *al dente* or tender but firm; rinse under cold water to remove starch and set aside.

In small oven-proof dish, set garlic cloves sprinkled with some olive oil. Bake in 350°F (180°C) oven until light golden brown. Remove from oven and crush into paste.

Prepare Hollandaise Sauce according to recipe. Blend in garlic paste and let stand.

Grill lamb chops over medium-high heat until medium-rare to medium. Just before ready to serve, rinse pasta under very hot water to reheat.

Divide pasta among six plates; place chops on top and spoon sauce over each. Sprinkle with chopped fresh parsley and serve.

Makes 6 servings.

Braised Lamb Shanks

I had Gems volunteers Debbie Farquhar and Glenna Crockford and their husbands, Robert and Jim, over for dinner and served this dish. It was a tremendous hit. Shanks require a lot of long, slow simmering, but there's a tremendous amount of flavor in this less expensive cut of lamb. Serve with roasted vegetables and mashed potatoes.

6	lamb shanks (about 4 lb/2 kg)	6
1 tbsp	vegetable oil	15 mL
2	onions, sliced	2
1-1/2 cups	beef stock	375 mL
2 tbsp	tomato paste	25 mL
2 tbsp	mint jelly	25 mL
1 tbsp	Worcestershire sauce	15 mL
1 tbsp	balsamic vinegar	15 mL
1 tsp	dried rosemary	5 mL
1/4 tsp	each salt and pepper	1 mL
	Chopped fresh parsley	

In large deep skillet over medium-high heat, heat oil; brown shanks, in batches, on all sides. Remove each browned shank to plate.

Add onions to skillet and cook, stirring, over medium heat for 2 to 3 minutes or until golden. Stir in onions, beef stock, tomato paste, mint jelly, Worcestershire, vinegar, rosemary, salt, and pepper; bring to boil over high heat, stirring and scraping any bits from bottom of skillet.

Return shanks to skillet with any accumulated juices, arranging in single layer and spooning some cooking liquid over them. Reduce heat to low; simmer, tightly covered, for 1-1/2 hours, or until shanks are very tender. Baste and turn shanks occasionally.

Using slotted spoon, remove shanks to serving dish; keep warm. Boil contents of skillet over high heat for a few minutes to reduce. Sprinkle shanks with parsley and serve with mashed potatoes. Spoon sauce over.

Makes 6 servings.

Glazed Pork Roast

Maureen Cole never seems to have the time to fuss in the kitchen. What with her successful business, softball games, and volunteer work, she is always on the go. So the following recipe is one of her clever ways of turning out a special meal with a minimum of effort.

TIP: You can find teriyaki baste-and-glaze sauce in most supermarkets.

3 lb	pork loin roast	1.5 kg
½ cup	teriyaki baste-and-glaze sauce	125 mL
2 tbsp	red current jelly	25 mL
1 tbsp	dry sherry	15 mL
1 tsp	grated fresh gingerroot	5 mL
⅛ tsp	ground cloves	½ mL

Pierce top of roast several times with fork. Place pork on rack in shallow roasting pan. Roast in 325°F (160°C) oven for 1 hour and 45 minutes, or until meat thermometer inserted into thickest part reaches 160°F (71°C).

Meanwhile, combine teriyaki baste-and-glaze sauce, jelly, sherry, gingerroot, and cloves. Brush pork with mixture every 10 minutes during last 30 minutes of cooking time. Remove pork to serving platter and let stand 10 minutes before carving.

Meanwhile, pour ½ cup (125 mL) water in roasting pan, stirring to combine with pan drippings; bring to boil and serve with sliced roast.

Makes 6 servings.

Ham and Cheese Strata

Make this layered dish the day before—and bake for a great brunch or light dinner with a salad.

16	slices bread, crusts removed	16
1-1/2 cups	chopped ham or bacon	375 mL
1-1/2 cups	grated Cheddar cheese	375 mL
6	eggs	6
2 cups	milk	500 mL
1/2 to 1 tsp	dry mustard	2 to 5 mL
1/2 tsp	each salt and pepper	2 mL
1/4 cup	each chopped onion and green pepper	50 mL
1 tsp	Worcestershire sauce	5 mL
Dash	hot pepper sauce	Dash
1/4 cup	butter	50 mL
1-1/2 cups	crushed cornflakes or crispy rice cereal	375 mL

Place one layer of bread (8 slices) in greased 13- x 9-inch (3.5-L) baking dish.

Sprinkle with chopped ham and grated cheese; place another layer of bread over ham and cheese.

In bowl, whisk eggs and milk together and add seasonings, onion, green pepper, Worcestershire, and hot pepper sauce.

Pour egg mixture over bread, cover with plastic wrap, and refrigerate overnight.

In saucepan, melt butter; remove from heat and add cereal. Sprinkle cereal mixture on top of baking dish. Bake in 350°F (180°C) oven for 1 hour or until cooked through. Let stand 10 minutes, then cut into squares.

Makes 6 servings.

Pork and Peppers

Here's another great recipe from Maureen Cole. Once you have all your ingredients assembled, this is a very quick dish to make.

1	pkg (5 oz/125 g) Oriental curly noodles	1
1 lb	pork tenderloin	500 g
3 tbsp	low-sodium soy sauce, divided	45 mL
1/2 cup	unsweetened orange juice	125 mL
2 tbsp	balsamic vinegar	25 mL
1 tsp	honey	5 mL
2 tsp	cornstarch	10 mL
1/4 tsp	freshly ground pepper	1 mL
	Vegetable cooking spray	
1-1/2 cups	each cubed red and yellow bell peppers	375 mL

Cook noodles according to package directions, omitting salt and fat. Drain and set aside.

Trim fat from pork and cut into 3/4-inch (2-cm) cubes. Combine pork and 1 tbsp (15 mL) of soy sauce; stir well and set aside.

Combine remaining soy sauce, juice, vinegar, honey, cornstarch, and pepper; stir well and set aside.

Coat large nonstick skillet with cooking spray and place over high heat. When hot, add pork mixture; stir-fry for 1-1/2 minutes or until browned. Remove pork from skillet; set aside. Add bell peppers to skillet; stir-fry for 2 minutes. Return pork to skillet; add juice mixture. Bring to boil and cook for 1 minute, stirring constantly. Add noodles; cook for 1 minute or until heated through.

Makes 4 servings.

Crustless Sausage Quiche

This dish, sometimes called a strata, makes a tasty brunch or light dinner. Best of all, it gets made the night before.

6	eggs, lightly beaten	6
2 cups	milk	500 mL
1 lb	bulk sausage (sausage meat removed from its casings), browned and drained	500 g
1/2 lb	Cheddar cheese, grated	250 g
1 tsp	dry mustard	5 mL
6	slices whole wheat bread, crusts removed and cubed	6

In bowl, combine eggs, milk, sausage, cheese, and mustard.

Place bread cubes in greased casserole; pour egg mixture over cubes.

Refrigerate for 24 hours. Bake in 325°F (160°C) oven for 1 hour or until cooked through. Let stand 5 minutes before serving.

Makes 6 servings.

Oven-Barbecued Spareribs

Everyone loves these zesty, sticky, wonderful ribs. This is a very forgiving recipe. I once totally forgot they were in the oven, covered on low, for over two hours. And they were still fabulous.

4 lb	spareribs	2 kg
2 tsp	salt	10 mL
1 cup	honey	250 mL
1 cup	ketchup	250 mL
1/2 cup	chili sauce	125 mL
1/2 cup	chopped onion	125 mL
2 tbsp	vinegar	25 mL
2 tbsp	steak sauce	25 mL
1 tbsp	prepared mustard	15 mL
2	cloves garlic, minced	2
1/2 tsp	pepper	2 mL

Cut ribs into serving-size pieces. Put in large saucepan with 1 tsp (5 mL) salt and enough boiling water to cover. Bring to boil; turn down heat, cover, and simmer for 30 minutes.

In saucepan, combine honey, ketchup, chili sauce, onion, vinegar, steak sauce, mustard, garlic, remaining salt, and pepper; bring to boil, turn down heat, and simmer for 10 minutes.

Drain spareribs well; put them into large shallow roasting pan in single layer, if possible. Pour honey mixture over. Bake in 400°F (200°C) oven for about 45 minutes or until ribs are very tender. Baste often with honey mixture and turn ribs occasionally. (A little water may be added near end of cooking time.)

Makes 4 to 6 servings.

Country Style Sausages and Potatoes

You couldn't ask for better comfort food than this delicious, one-pot meal.

1 lb	sweet Italian sausages	500 g
2 tbsp	extra virgin olive oil	25 mL
2	cloves garlic, chopped	2
1 lb	onions, sliced very thin	500 g
1 lb	fresh ripe plum tomatoes	500 g
6	bay leaves, cut in half	6
1-1/2 lb	new potatoes, peeled and cut into 1-1/2-inch (4-cm) wedges	750 g
	Salt and pepper	

Pierce sausages a few times with fork and place them in saucepan with oil, garlic, and sliced onions. Cook, covered, on medium-low heat.

Meanwhile, wash tomatoes and cut into wedges; add to saucepan.

When onions are tender, uncover pan; increase to high heat and cook, stirring frequently, until onions turn light golden brown.

Add bay leaves, cover, and return to medium heat. Cook for another 10 to 12 minutes, stirring occasionally. Add potatoes and salt and pepper to taste. Cover and continue to cook until potatoes are tender. Remove bay leaves.

Makes 4 to 6 servings.

Tortière

Catherine Mossop is president of Mossop Cornelissen & Associates, and she sits on the board of Gems of Hope and Amerasia Network. As a student at university in Quebec, Catherine lived in a house apartment above a large French family. The mother made these Tortières every December and gave her one: "I had never eaten one better and asked for her recipe. We had to break it down into something more manageable than the dozen she made."

Pastry for double-crust pie (10 inch/25 cm)

Filling:

³/₄ cup	chopped onions	175 mL
¹/₄ cup	diced celery	50 mL
1	clove garlic, crushed	1
³/₄ lb	each ground pork and ground veal	375 g
2 cups	chopped fresh parsley	500 mL
¹/₂ tsp	each dry sage and salt	2 mL
Pinch	each fresh scraped nutmeg, ground cloves, and ground cinnamon	Pinch
	Freshly ground pepper	
¹/₄ to ¹/₂ cup	bread crumbs	50 to 125 mL

TIP: Tortière tastes best when left to stand one day in the refrigerator prior to baking and serving. It freezes very well too. Let stand in refrigerator to thaw overnight before baking. Serve it with a green salad and French bread, accompanied by a Beaujolais Nouveau.

FILLING:

In large heavy lightly greased skillet, sauté onions, celery, and garlic until transparent. Add pork, veal, parsley, sage, salt, nutmeg, cloves, cinnamon, and pepper to taste. Sauté over medium-low heat until meat is cooked and liquid has evaporated. Mix in enough bread crumbs to create moist but not dry texture. Allow to cool.

Pour filling into prepared pie crust. Cover with top crust; seal and flute edges. Cut a few slashes in top to let steam escape.

Bake in 425°F (220°C) oven for 10 minutes then lower temperature to 325°F (160°C) and bake until crust is golden brown. Makes one large 10-inch (25-cm) double-crust pie or two 8-inch (20-cm) double-crust pies.

Veal Oscar

Once you've made the Hollandaise, the rest of this dish is dead easy.

4	veal slices (each 5 oz/140 g)	4
1 cup	all-purpose flour	250 mL
	Salt and pepper	
	Butter	
¼ cup	crab meat	50 mL
12	cooked asparagus spears	12
	Hollandaise Sauce	
	(recipe follows)	

Prepare Hollandaise Sauce (recipe follows).

Pound veal thin (or have your butcher do it), dredge in flour, and salt and pepper to taste.

In skillet, heat some butter and sauté veal a few minutes on each side.

Remove veal to serving platter; place some crab meat on each piece of veal and top each serving with 3 asparagus spears. Serve with Hollandaise Sauce.

Hollandaise Sauce:

This is a more foolproof method of preparing this sauce then the traditional version. (This sauce can also be bought in jars at most food shops.)

½ lb	butter, very cold and cut in pieces	250 g
2	egg yolks	2
1 tbsp	fresh lemon juice	15 mL
¼ tsp	salt	1 mL
Pinch	cayenne pepper	Pinch
	Boiling water	
	(approx. 4 tsp/20 mL)	

In heavy bowl, cream butter thoroughly; gradually beat in egg yolks and lemon juice. Add salt and cayenne. Set bowl over hot water and stir constantly until mixture thickens slightly. Remove from hot water until you are almost ready to use.

At this final moment, add boiling water, 1 tsp (5 mL) at a time, stirring constantly, until sauce is thickened. Stop adding boiling water as soon as sauce is right thickness.

Makes 4 servings.

Screwdriver Veal

Substitute chicken cutlets for the veal for a change of flavor.

1 cup	all-purpose flour	250 mL
1/2 tsp	salt	2 mL
1/4 tsp	pepper	1 mL
	Paprika	
6	veal cutlets	6
1/4 cup	olive oil	50 mL
3 tbsp	butter	45 mL
2	cloves garlic, minced	2
3/4 cup	orange juice	175 mL
3/4 cup	vodka	175 mL
2 tbsp	chopped parsley	25 mL
Pinch	cayenne pepper	Pinch

In plastic bag, combine flour, salt, pepper, and enough paprika to lightly color flour pink. Add cutlets, one at a time, and toss to coat completely.

In 10-inch (25-cm) skillet, heat oil, butter, and garlic. Add cutlets and cook for 3 to 5 minutes per side or until browned.

Remove to platter and drain oil from pan. Reduce heat and add juice, vodka, parsley, and cayenne pepper to pan; stir to scrape up pan drippings. Sprinkle some flour in pan and stir to thicken sauce.

Immediately add cutlets; return heat to high and cook for 1 more minute.

Makes 6 servings.

Veal Parmesan

This traditional favorite is best served with crusty bread and a green salad.

1/2 cup	bread crumbs	125 mL
1/4 cup	grated Parmesan cheese	50 mL
1 tsp	dried oregano	5 mL
1 tsp	salt	5 mL
1/2 tsp	black pepper	2 mL
2 lb	veal cutlets, sliced 1/8-inch (3-mm) thick	1 kg
2	eggs, beaten	2
3/4 cup	vegetable oil	175 mL
1/2 lb	mozzarella cheese, sliced	250 g
1	can (14 oz/398 mL) spaghetti sauce	1

Mix bread crumbs with Parmesan, oregano, salt, and pepper.

Wipe veal dry with paper towels and dip into beaten eggs; coat well on both sides with bread crumb mixture.

In skillet, slowly heat vegetable oil and sauté cutlets, a few at a time, until golden brown. Place cooked cutlets in baking dish and top with mozzarella. Pour spaghetti sauce over.

Bake in 175°F (80°C) for 10 to 15 minutes.

Makes 6 servings.

Veal Scallops with Gorgonzola Sauce

Add a touch of elegance to dinner with this main dish.

6	veal scallops	6
	(each about 3-1/2 oz/100 g)	
1 cup	all-purpose flour	250 mL
3 tbsp	olive oil	45 mL
1/2 cup	brandy	125 mL
1/2 cup	unsalted butter, cut into bits	125 mL
1/4 lb	Gorgonzola, crumbled	125 g
1/2 cup	heavy cream	125 mL
	Pepper	

Pat veal dry and pound thinner if too thick. Dredge veal in flour, shaking off any excess. In skillet, heat oil and sauté veal over medium-high heat for 30 to 60 seconds per side. Transfer veal to platter and keep warm.

Add brandy to skillet and deglaze pan, scraping up brown bits on bottom and sides. Over moderate heat, reduce mixture by half.

Reduce heat to medium low; whisk in butter and cook, whisking, until butter melts. Stir in Gorgonzola and cream. Cook sauce, whisking, until cheese is melted.

Season with pepper to taste. Top veal with sauce and serve.

Makes 6 servings.

Chicken Adobo

This recipe is wonderful, very easy, and one of my favorites. It came to me from a Philippine friend. Gems has a program in the Philippines, where apparently "Adobo" means stew. The soy sauce gives the dish a pleasant salty flavor. Low-sodium (lite) soy sauce can certainly be used.

2 tbsp	vegetable oil	25 mL
1	onion, sliced into rings	1
3 lb	skinless chicken (thighs or breast halves)	1.5 kg
1/3 cup	soy sauce	75 mL
1/4 cup	fresh lemon juice	50 mL
2 to 3	large garlic cloves	2 to 3
2 tsp	pepper	10 mL
1	bay leaf	1

In skillet, heat oil and sauté onion until translucent.

Add chicken, soy sauce, lemon juice, garlic, pepper, and bay leaf. Cook covered over medium heat for 30 minutes.

Remove lid and cook for another 15 minutes. Remove bay leaf. Serve with cooked rice.

Makes 4 to 6 servings.

Chicken Cacciatore

TIP: Serve with spaghetti and garlic bread. Use a large platter and put cooked spaghetti around the plate leaving a hole in the middle to pile the chicken. Top with sauce and serve. A Caesar salad would be wonderful with this dish.

Chicken Cacciatore is an Italian chicken stew. To serve a gang, simply double this recipe.

1	large onion, sliced	1
4 tbsp	olive oil (divided)	50 mL
3 lb	chicken pieces (breast, legs, or thighs)	1.5 kg
½ cup	all-purpose flour	125 mL
1 tsp	salt	5 mL
½ tsp	pepper	2 mL
½ tsp	marjoram	2 mL
⅛ tsp	garlic powder	1/2 mL
2 cups	canned tomatoes	500 mL
1 cup	coarsely chopped green peppers	250 mL
½ cup	dry white wine	125 mL
	Salt and pepper	

In skillet, sauté onion in 2 tbsp (25 mL) of olive oil.

Meanwhile, toss chicken pieces in a bag with seasoned flour (flour, salt, pepper, marjoram, and garlic powder).

Add remaining oil to pan and heat. Add floured chicken and cook until well browned. Add tomatoes and peppers, cover, and cook for 20 minutes over medium heat, stirring occasionally. Add wine and salt and pepper to taste; cook gently for 10 minutes more or until tender.

Makes 4 servings.

Chicken Cordon Bleu

Serve this at your next dinner party. It's actually quite easy and will win you bouquets. Double the recipe to make an excellent buffet dish.

8	boneless skinless chicken breasts	8
8	slices cooked ham	8
8	slices Swiss cheese	8
3 tbsp	minced fresh parsley	45 mL
	Pepper	
1	egg, beaten	1
1/2 cup	bread crumbs	125 mL
1/2 cup	butter	125 mL
1	can (10 oz/284 mL) Cheddar cheese soup	1
1 cup	sour cream	250 mL
1/3 cup	dry sherry	75 mL

Place each chicken breast on sheet of waxed paper and, using mallet, flatten to 1/4-inch (5-mm) thickness. Place 1 slice each ham and cheese in center of each piece; sprinkle with parsley and pepper to taste. Roll up each chicken breast and secure with wooden pick. Dip each into beaten egg and coat well with bread crumbs.

In heavy skillet, melt butter; brown chicken pieces. Place chicken in 13- x 9-inch (3.5-L) baking dish, reserving drippings.

Add cheese soup, sour cream, and sherry to drippings in skillet. Stir well and pour over chicken.

Bake, uncovered, in 350°F (180°C) oven for 40 to 45 minutes.

Makes 8 servings.

Chicken with Creamy Parmesan Sauce

Make a memorable dish that is very easy, attractive, and delicious.

4	boneless skinless chicken breasts	4
1 tbsp	butter	15 mL
¼ to ½ tsp	ground thyme	1 to 2 mL
⅔ cup	mayonnaise	150 mL
⅓ cup	sour cream	75 mL
⅓ cup	freshly grated Parmesan cheese	75 mL

In skillet, melt butter and sauté chicken for 5 minutes on each side or until light brown.

Arrange chicken in shallow baking dish and sprinkle ground thyme over each breast.

In bowl, combine mayonnaise, sour cream, and Parmesan cheese. Place some mayonnaise mixture on each chicken breast. Bake at 350°F (180°C) for about 40 minutes or until golden brown.

Makes 4 servings.

Barbequed Lemon Chicken

Serve this perfect light summer dish with grilled vegetables and a simple green salad.

¼ cup	lemon juice	50 mL
¼ cup	olive or vegetable oil	50 mL
2 tsp	chopped, fresh thyme	10 mL
	(or ½ tsp/2 mL dried)	
1 tsp	black peppercorns	5 mL
4	boneless skinless chicken breasts	4

In measuring cup, combine lemon juice, oil, and thyme. Crush peppercorns; add to lemon mixture.

Place chicken in shallow baking dish; pour mixture over, turning to coat completely. Refrigerate for 1 to 3 hours (or overnight), turning chicken occasionally.

Remove chicken from marinade and grill over medium-high heat for about 25 minutes or until chicken is done and juices run clear.

Makes 4 servings.

Easy Chicken Divan

You can substitute turkey for the chicken in this recipe. It's a good way to use up the holiday bird.

2	bunches broccoli, in bite-size pieces	2
2 cups	sliced cooked chicken	500 mL
2	cans (each 10 oz/284 mL) cream of mushroom soup	2
1 cup	mayonnaise	250 mL
1/2 cup	grated Cheddar cheese	125 mL
1 tsp	lemon juice	5 mL
1/2 tsp	curry powder	2 mL
1/2 cup	soft bread crumbs	125 mL
1 tbsp	butter, melted	15 mL

Place broccoli in 9- x 7-inch (2-L) baking dish and place chicken on top.

In bowl, mix soup, mayonnaise, cheese, lemon juice, and curry powder; pour over chicken.

In another bowl, mix bread crumbs with melted butter and sprinkle over sauce in baking dish. Bake in 350°F (180°C) oven for 20 minutes.

Makes 4 servings.

Piccata of Turkey with Yogurt and Apricots

I picked up this recipe years ago from a gal I met in St. Lucia. "Piccata" is an Italian term for small, thinly sliced meat—usually veal—and sometimes called scaloppini. This version with turkey is especially nice.

6	dried apricots	6
6	thin slices turkey breast, flattened with mallet	6
	All-purpose flour seasoned with salt and pepper	
1/4 cup	unsalted butter	50 mL
1 tbsp	finely chopped onions	15 mL
1/4 cup	port	50 mL
3 tbsp	plain yogurt	45 mL
3 tbsp	heavy cream	45 mL
	Salt and freshly ground pepper	

Soften apricots in small amount of hot water.

Dredge slices of turkey in seasoned flour. In sauté pan over medium heat, melt 2 tbsp (25 mL) of the butter and sauté turkey slices for 2 to 3 minutes per side or until lightly browned. Remove and set aside.

Drain half of fat from pan; add onion and sauté until golden.

Add port to deglaze pan; add drained apricots and reduce liquid to half. Add yogurt, cream, and salt and pepper to taste. Reduce to half again or until thick enough to coat wooden spoon. Add remaining butter to sauce and shake pan back and forth to incorporate butter (this will give a gloss to the sauce). On serving plate, pour sauce over turkey. Serve 3 piccata per person.

Makes 2 servings.

Tandoori Chicken

Glenna Crockford submitted this dish. I've been making it for years in very large batches for parties. Because it's prepared the day before, it makes entertaining a lot easier.

8	pieces skinless chicken (or 10 small)	8
	Salt	
1 cup	plain yogurt	250 mL
2 tbsp	chopped fresh ginger	25 mL
	(or 1-1/2 tsp/7 mL ground)	
2 tbsp	lemon juice	25 mL
3	cloves garlic, finely chopped	3
1 tsp	chili powder	5 mL
	Paprika	

With sharp knife make slashes in chicken pieces. Rub salt into each piece. Place in baking dish.

In bowl, mix yogurt, ginger, lemon juice, garlic, chili powder, and paprika to taste. Pour over chicken, coating each piece. Cover and refrigerate overnight (10 to 12 hours).

Grill over medium-high heat for 15 minutes per side or until juices run clear when chicken is pierced.

Makes 6 to 8 servings.

Turkey and Vegetable Casserole

Here's another great way to use up leftover turkey (or chicken).

4 cups	cooked broccoli	1 L
1 cup	sliced, crisply cooked carrots	250 mL
1 cup	thinly sliced green peppers (optional)	250 mL
1-1/2 cups	diced cooked turkey	375 mL
1	can (10 oz/284 mL) cheese and broccoli soup	1
1/3 cup	milk	75 mL
1 tbsp	melted butter	15 mL
2 tbsp	bread crumbs	25 mL

In 12-cup (3-L) casserole dish, arrange vegetables and top with turkey.

In bowl, mix soup and milk; pour over turkey and vegetables.

In small bowl, mix melted butter and bread crumbs; sprinkle over casserole.

Bake in 450°F (230°C) oven for 15 minutes or until heated through.

Makes 4 servings.

Fish and Seafood

Baked Haddock

This is a great fast and low-fat recipe submitted by Maureen Cole. Moe is typical of many of today's independent businesswomen: she works hard, plays hard, and doesn't have a lot of time for the kitchen.

4	haddock fillets (each 4 oz/115 g) or any other firm fish	4
½ cup	fresh lime juice	125 mL
1	can (19 oz/540 g) diced tomatoes, undrained	1
1 tbsp	dried onion	15 mL
1 tbsp	dried parsley	15 mL

Place fish in shallow baking dish.

In bowl, combine lime juice, tomatoes, onion, and parsley. Pour mixture over fish.

Bake, uncovered, in 400°F (200°C) oven for 15 to 20 minutes or until fish flakes easily with fork.

Makes 4 servings.

Grilled Salmon Steaks

Use the reserved marinade to baste the steaks on the barbecue.

6	salmon steaks	6
1 cup	dry vermouth	250 mL
2/3 cup	butter, melted (or oil)	150 mL
1/4 cup	lemon juice	50 mL
2 tbsp	finely chopped onion	25 mL
2 tsp	salt	10 mL
1/4 tsp	each marjoram, pepper, and thyme	1 mL
Pinch	sage	Pinch

Place salmon in shallow dish.

In bowl, combine vermouth, butter, lemon juice, onion, salt, marjoram, pepper, thyme, and sage. Pour over salmon. Cover and let stand at room temperature for about 4 hours, turning steaks occasionally.

Remove steaks, reserving marinade. Cook steaks on greased grill 4 inches (10 cm) from hot coals or on high setting for about 8 minutes. Turn and cook other side. Baste with marinade during cooking.

Makes 6 servings.

Cajun Shrimp

TIP: **This is a spicy dish, so try serving it with rice and a salad or sliced tomatoes.**

After you've prepared this scrumptious simple dish once, it will become one of your favorites. Have the rest of your meal ready before you start as this cooks quickly and shouldn't be left sitting.

1-1/2 cups	margarine	375 mL
1 tsp	each minced garlic, salt, cayenne pepper, dried basil, and black pepper	5 mL
1/2 tsp	each white pepper and dried thyme	2 mL
3/4 cup	white wine	175 mL
1 cup	chopped green onions	250 mL
1/2 lb	crab meat, picked over	250 g
1 lb	shrimp, peeled and deveined	500 g

In large saucepan, melt margarine; add garlic and spices. Cook until margarine starts bubbling.

Add wine, green onions, crab meat, and shrimp. Cook until shrimp are opaque. Do not overcook.

Makes 4 to 6 servings.

Oven-Poached Salmon

Here's a wonderful way to prepare salmon. I first had this dish in British Columbia about sixteen years ago and have been preparing it ever since. It can be cooked on the grill just as easily as in the oven.

1-1/2 to 2 lb	salmon fillet	750 g to 1 kg
2 tsp	butter	10 mL
	Few sliced onion rings	
1/2	lemon, cut in slices	1/2
1 tsp	capers	5 mL
	Lemon wedges	

Fold very long piece of foil in thirds; unfold one third. Place salmon (skin-side down) on double thickness of foil leaving at least 1/2 inch to 1 inch (1 to 2.5 cm) around edge.

Dot salmon with butter. Place a few onion rings and lemon slices over fillet; top with capers.

Fold last third of foil over fillet and double fold around edges to seal. Bake in 400°F (200°C) oven for 10 minutes for every inch (2.5 cm) of thickness of fish. (Cooking time will usually be 10 to 15 minutes.) Serve with lemon wedges.

Makes 4 servings.

TIP: If you decide to grill the salmon, prepare and wrap in foil as directed and grill over medium-high heat for 10 to 15 minutes (approximately 10 minutes to the inch/2.5 cm). Grill a few vegetables to accompany the salmon.

Crab Cakes with Lime Sauce

There are many crab cake recipes around but this one has a lime sauce that makes it truly delicious.

²/₃ cup	mayonnaise	150 mL
1 tbsp	fresh lime juice	15 mL
¹/₄ to ¹/₂ tsp	freshly ground black pepper	1 to 2 mL
12 oz	flaked crab meat	300 g
¹/₂ cup	bread crumbs	125 mL
2 oz	chopped pimiento	50 g
2 tbsp	chopped green onion	25 mL
	Lime Sauce (recipe follows)	

In large bowl, mix mayonnaise, lime juice, and pepper. Add crab meat, bread crumbs, pimiento, and green onion.

Form mixture into 8 patties. In skillet, heat some margarine or oil and fry crab cakes for 3 minutes on each side. Serve hot with Lime Sauce.

Makes 4 servings.

Lime Sauce:

¹/₂ cup	mayonnaise	125 mL
¹/₄ cup	sour cream	50 mL
1 tbsp	fresh lime juice	15 mL
2 tsp	lime zest	10 mL

In bowl, mix mayonnaise, sour cream, lime juice, and zest. Serve with crab cakes.

Makes ¾ cup (175 mL) sauce.

Fettuccine with Scallops in Cream and Garlic Sauce

It's best, if possible, to use fresh pasta—in this case fettuccine. This dish is well worth the effort.

1 lb	fresh fettuccine	500 g
¼ cup	clarified butter (see sidebar)	50 mL
2	cloves garlic, finely minced	2
½ cup	finely diced onion	125 mL
1 tsp	dried basil	5 mL
1 tsp	Worcestershire sauce	5 mL
Pinch	crushed, dried red chili peppers	Pinch
1 lb	scallops	500 g
¼ cup	dry white wine	50 mL
1 cup	whipping cream	250 mL
	Salt and pepper	
1 tbsp	chopped fresh parsley	15 mL

TIP: **Melt butter slowly until it separates. The clear liquid is clarified butter. Spoon the clear butter off and set aside. Discard the cloudy part. Clarified butter is called for in a lot of seafood dishes.**

In large pot of boiling water, cook fettuccine until *al dente* (tender but firm). Drain and keep warm.

In large skillet, heat clarified butter; sauté garlic for 2 minutes (being careful not to burn it) over medium heat. Discard garlic; add onion, basil, Worcestershire sauce, and chili peppers and sauté until onion is tender.

Add scallops and continue to cook until scallops turn opaque. Remove scallops to warm plate. Add wine to pan and stir to deglaze; add whipping cream and salt and pepper to taste. Divide pasta into four servings; top with scallops and wine and cream sauce. Sprinkle with fresh parsley.

Makes 4 servings.

Seafood Newburg

TIP: **Serve over rice, noodles, or in a puff pastry shell.**

This dish is for a special party and it's very quick to prepare. This recipe is from Sharon, a nurse I met in St. Lucia, who was there with CUSO, on a two-year contract with the hospital.

1/2 cup	butter	125 mL
3/4 cup	all-purpose flour	175 mL
2 tsp	salt	10 mL
4 cups	milk	1 L
3 tbsp	tomato paste	45 mL
1 tbsp	lemon juice	15 mL
2 tsp	Worcestershire sauce	10 mL
2 tbsp	butter	25 mL
2	cans (each 10 oz/284 mL) button mushrooms	2
1 lb	scallops	500 g
1/2 lb	lobster meat (canned or fresh)	250 g
1/2 lb	medium-sized cooked shelled shrimp	250 g

In large saucepan, melt 1/2 cup (125 mL) butter. Stir in flour and salt; add milk. Stir and cook until mixture boils and thickens. Add tomato paste, lemon juice, and Worcestershire sauce. Remove from heat and set aside.

Melt 2 tbsp (25 mL) butter in separate pan. Add mushrooms and sauté until golden brown. Stir into sauce.

In separate medium saucepan, combine scallops with enough water to cover. Bring to boil and simmer for 5 minutes. Drain and cut large scallops in half; add to sauce.

Drain lobster and shrimp. Break lobster into bite-size pieces, removing any cartilage. Add lobster and shrimp to sauce and heat over low heat (or transfer to casserole to be heated when needed). Heat, covered, in 350°F (180°C) oven for 30 minutes or until hot.

Makes 8 to 10 servings.

Seafood Omelette for Two

This is wonderful served with fresh cooked asparagus and a chilled Chablis.

6	eggs	6
1/2 cup	milk	125 mL
2 tbsp	grated Parmesan cheese	25 mL
1/4 cup	grated Cheddar or Swiss cheese	50 mL
3	slices mozzarella cheese	3
1/2 cup	cooked shrimp, scallops, or crab meat	125 mL
1 tbsp	sour cream (optional)	15 mL

TIP: Some other filling suggestions include broccoli and cheese, mushrooms, or spinach.

In blender, blend eggs, milk, and Parmesan cheese on high for 30 seconds. Pour into heated buttered omelette pan or medium-size skillet.

Add Cheddar and mozzarella cheeses. Cover loosely with aluminum foil and cook slowly. Omelette will puff up like a soufflé. Add seafood filling and sour cream (if using). Fold out onto platter and serve.

Makes 2 servings.

Sole Amandine

Serve this all-time favorite with baked potatoes and a colorful coleslaw.

2	sole fillets (each 6 to 8 oz/170 to 225 g)	2
	All-purpose flour for dredging	
½ cup	butter	125 mL
	Salt and pepper	
½ cup	white wine	125 mL
1 tbsp	fresh lemon juice	15 mL
¼ cup	sliced almonds, roasted	50 mL
	Chopped fresh parsley	

Dredge sole fillets in flour. In skillet, heat ¼ cup (50 mL) butter and sauté fillets. (Sauté side from which skin has been removed first and fish will hold together better.) Season with salt and pepper to taste.

Turn fillets and deglaze pan with white wine and lemon juice. Add almonds and parsley to taste. Remove fish to plate and keep warm.

Reduce cooking liquid by half. Add remaining butter, remove from heat, and swirl to incorporate into sauce.

Pour sauce over fish and serve.

Makes 2 servings.

Thai Shrimp

Thai dishes are very flavorful. This one may become a big hit with your family and friends.

	Canola oil	
2	cloves garlic, minced	2
1 tbsp	grated fresh gingerroot	15 mL
	Lemon grass	
3	green onions	3
1	jalapeño pepper, chopped	1
1 lb	shrimp	500 g
½ cup	coconut milk or coconut cream	125 mL
	Salt and pepper	
	Chopped fresh Italian parsley	

TIP: Have rice and a salad ready before you start this dish as it comes together very fast and you'll want to serve it immediately.

In wok or skillet, heat some canola oil and sauté garlic, ginger, lemon grass, green onions, and jalapeño for 2 minutes.

Add shrimp and stir-fry for 1 minute. Add coconut milk and cook for 1 to 2 minutes.

Add salt and pepper to taste and serve, sprinkled with parsley, over rice.

Makes 4 servings.

Vegetables and Side Dishes

Baked Beans

This quick and easy bean bake is great at any barbecue. The recipe is from my sister-in-law Elaine, who used to volunteer at a children's home in Scarborough, Ontario. Kids love this side dish.

3	cans (each 14 oz/398 mL) beans in tomato sauce	3
1 cup	ketchup	250 mL
3/4 cup	chopped onion	175 mL
1/4 cup	packed brown sugar	50 mL
1-1/2 tsp	Worcestershire sauce	7 mL

In 12-cup (3 L) casserole, combine beans, ketchup, onion, brown sugar, and Worcestershire sauce. Bake, uncovered, in 350°F (180°C) oven for 1-1/2 hours or until bubbling throughout and well browned around edges.

Makes 6 to 8 servings.

Opposite: Barbequed Lemon Chicken (page 81)
Overleaf: Grilled Salmon Steaks (page 87)

Cabbage Sautéed with Cumin

This is a dish from an old friend and a true supporter of many fine charities. Melissa Luke does wonderful things with vegetables.

3 tbsp	oil	45 mL
1	large onion, thinly sliced	1
1	medium cabbage, cored and shredded	1
1/2 tsp	dried thyme	2 mL
1/2 tsp	cumin seed, crushed	2 mL
1	clove garlic, finely chopped	1
1-1/2 tsp	salt	7 mL
	Freshly ground pepper	

In skillet, heat oil over medium heat. Add onion and sauté until transparent. Add cabbage, thyme, and cumin seed.

Increase heat to medium-high and sauté for about 10 minutes, stirring frequently to prevent burning. Add garlic and sauté for 1 minute. Add salt and pepper to taste and serve immediately.

Makes 4 servings.

Overleaf: Stir-Fry Ginger Broccoli (page 106)
Opposite: Chocolate Swirl Cheesecake (page 111)

Gingered Carrots

This is another of Melissa Luke's veggie dishes and it is very easy to make.

2 tbsp	unsalted butter	25 mL
1/2	onion, finely chopped	1/2
1 lb	carrots, peeled and sliced	500 g
1/2 cup	water	125 mL
1/4 cup	maple syrup	50 mL
1 tbsp	crystallized ginger, finely chopped	15 mL
	(or 2 tsp/10 mL grated fresh gingerroot)	
1/2 tsp	salt	2 mL
1 tsp	finely chopped fresh parsley	5 mL

In skillet over medium heat, melt butter and sauté onion until transparent. Add carrots, water, maple syrup, ginger, and salt. Cook for about 30 minutes, stirring occasionally, until carrots are just tender. Sprinkle with parsley and serve immediately.

Makes 6 servings.

Grilled Vegetables

This is another wonderful recipe from Debbie Farquhar (one of our dedicated volunteers). She suggests placing a bottle of extra virgin olive oil on the table, for your guests to pass around.

2	medium zucchini, sliced diagonally	2
1	large red pepper (whole)	1
1	medium sweet potato, peeled and cut into 1-inch (2.5-cm) slices	1
1	medium eggplant, quartered lengthwise	1
1	large red onion, quartered	1
½ cup	extra virgin olive oil	125 mL
¼ cup	balsamic vinegar	50 mL
3	large cloves garlic, minced	3
¼ cup	chopped fresh rosemary	50 mL
¼ cup	chopped fresh basil	50 mL

In large bowl, combine all ingredients except basil. Mix well, coating all vegetables and let stand for 2 hours or overnight in refrigerator.

Grill on greased grill over medium heat until tender. Return pieces to bowl as they are cooked.

Cook red pepper until skin is blackened; cool and remove skin and seeds; cut into 2-inch (5-cm) pieces.

When all vegetables have cooled enough to handle, cut into bite-size pieces and toss with fresh basil.

Makes 6 servings.

TIP: These grilled vegetables are excellent served with Beef Brochettes (page 60) or Steak with Herb-Spice Rub (page 57).

TIP: This dish is served at room temperature, so it can be made ahead of time. The vegetable list used is just a guideline; add or omit anything you like.

O'Brien Potatoes

This is a wonderful way to serve the old spud and the whole family will love it.

1 tbsp	vegetable oil	15 mL
4	potatoes, peeled and diced	4
	Salt and pepper	
1	onion, peeled and diced	1
3	slices bacon, browned and diced	3
1 tbsp	chopped fresh parsley	15 mL

In large skillet, heat oil; add potatoes, and salt and pepper to taste. Partially cover and cook for 6 to 7 minutes over medium heat.

Add onion and bacon; cook for 3 to 4 minutes, uncovered, over medium-high heat. Sprinkle with parsley and serve.

Makes 4 servings.

Orange Curried Rice

Here's a nice savory side dish that can be doubled to make a good buffet item.

¼ cup	butter	50 mL
½ cup	chopped onion	125 mL
1 cup	uncooked rice	250 mL
2 tsp	curry powder	10 mL
1 cup	orange juice	250 mL
1 cup	chicken broth	250 mL
½ cup	seedless raisins	125 mL
1 tsp	salt	5 mL
1	bay leaf	1

In heavy saucepan, melt butter and sauté onions until soft. Stir in rice and curry powder; cook, stirring, for two minutes.

Add orange juice, broth, raisins, salt, and bay leaf; stir with fork. Bring to boil; lower heat and simmer, covered, for 20 minutes. Remove bay leaf and serve.

Makes 6 servings.

Peach Chutney

Serve this chutney with lamb or cold meats. It's also wonderful with the Braided Sausage Ring on page 14. I use dark plums as I prefer the color of the finished product.

4 lb	peaches, plums, or combination	2 kg
4 cups	cider vinegar	1 L
2 lb	dark brown sugar	1 kg
1 cup	seedless raisins	250 mL
½ cup	chopped onion	125 mL
½ cup	chopped preserved ginger	125 mL
2	cloves garlic, minced	2
1 to 2 tbsp	chili powder	15 to 25 mL
1 tbsp	mustard seed	15 mL
1-½ tsp	salt	7 mL
1 tsp	curry powder	5 mL
3 tbsp	mixed pickling spices (tied in cheesecloth bag)	45 mL

Slice peeled peaches or other fruit. In Dutch oven or bowl, mix fruit with cider vinegar, brown sugar, raisins, onion, ginger, garlic, chili powder, mustard seed, salt, curry powder, and pickling spices in bag. Cover and let stand overnight.

Turn into heavy pot and simmer, uncovered, over medium heat, stirring frequently to prevent scorching, until chutney is of desired consistency. This cooking process will take about 1-½ hours. (When mixture thickly coats spoon, it is done. Chutney will continue to thicken as it cools in jars.)

Remove spice bag and ladle chutney into sterilized jars. Seal immediately.

Makes about 10 cups (2.5 L).

Roasted Cauliflower

When buying cauliflower, look for compact, firm, white to creamy-white florets. Avoid any that are trimmed or brownish. Leaves should be firm and green.

2 tbsp	olive oil	25 mL
2	cloves garlic, thinly sliced	2
Pinch	red pepper flakes	Pinch
Pinch	dried rosemary	Pinch
1	head cauliflower, cut in florets	1
	Salt and pepper	

In deep saucepan, heat olive oil and sauté garlic, pepper flakes, and rosemary. Add cauliflower and toss. Add salt and pepper to taste.

Transfer to roasting pan and roast in 375°F (190°C) oven for 30 minutes or until tender-crisp.

Makes 4 servings.

Marg's Scalloped Potatoes

This is a make-ahead dish from Marg Munro-McCall, and any leftovers can easily be reheated the next day.

3	large (or 6 medium) potatoes, peeled and thinly sliced	3
1	onion, peeled and thinly sliced	1
2 cups	Medium White Sauce (recipe follows)	500 mL
	Salt and pepper	
	Chopped fresh parsley	
1 cup	buttered bread crumbs (use day-old bread)	250 mL
1 cup	grated Cheddar cheese	250 mL

Boil sliced potatoes in salted water for 8 to 10 minutes or just until barely tender.

In greased 6-cup (1.5 L) casserole, layer potatoes, onion slices, and white sauce, sprinkling potatoes with salt, pepper, and parsley to taste. Top with bread crumbs and cheese; bake, uncovered, in 375°F (190°C) oven for 45 minutes to 1 hour or until topping is golden and potatoes are bubbling.

Makes 6 servings.

Medium White Sauce:

¹⁄₄ cup	butter	50 mL
¹⁄₄ cup	all-purpose flour	50 mL
¹⁄₄ tsp	dry mustard	1 mL
1 tsp	salt	5 mL
	Pepper	
2 cups	milk	500 mL
	Chopped fresh parsley	

In saucepan, melt butter. Stir in flour, mustard, salt, and pepper to taste. Mix well until all flour is coated with butter. Remove from heat.

Gradually stir in milk. Return to medium heat and cook, stirring frequently, for about 5 minutes or until thickened. Sprinkle with chopped fresh parsley.

Makes about 2 cups (500 mL) sauce.

Stir-Fry Ginger Broccoli

When buying broccoli, look for firm compact clusters of small flower buds and thin stalks. They should be dark blue-green. Avoid yellow or limp heads and split bottom stalks.

1 lb	broccoli	500 g
1 inch	fresh ginger, sliced thinly	2.5 cm
½ tsp	salt	2 mL
½ tsp	sesame oil	2 mL

Trim and peel broccoli stalks. Discard tough ends. Separate top into florets. In large pot of boiling water, cook broccoli for 3 minutes or just until tender-crisp; drain and put in cold water to stop cooking process.

In wok or heavy skillet, stir-fry ginger slices. Add salt and drained broccoli. Stir-fry (adding a bit of water if necessary). Add sesame oil, toss, and serve.

Makes 4 servings.

Yam and Cranberry Casserole

Here's one of my favorite side dishes, particularly for fall and winter festive gatherings.

4 cups	thinly sliced, peeled yam halves	1 L
1 cup	whole raw cranberries	250 mL
¾ cup	finely sliced onion	175 mL
1-½ cups	heavy cream	375 mL
1	egg, lightly beaten	1
½ tsp	salt	2 mL
¼ tsp	pepper (fresh ground if possible)	1 mL
	Nutmeg	
¼ cup	grated Parmesan cheese	50 mL

In oven-proof casserole, combine yams, cranberries, and onion.

In separate bowl, mix cream, egg, salt, pepper, and nutmeg to taste. Pour over yam-cranberry mixture and mix thoroughly. Bake, uncovered, in 375°F (190°C) oven for 20 minutes. Cover and bake for another 25 to 30 minutes.

Remove cover, sprinkle with Parmesan cheese, and return to oven for 5 minutes or until cheese melts.

Makes 6 servings.

Vegetable Supreme

This is another dish from my sister-in-law Elaine.

1	small cauliflower head, broken up	1
1	pkg (10 oz/284 g) frozen baby carrots	1
1	pkg (10 oz/284 g) frozen brussels sprouts	1
1	can (10 oz/284 mL) button mushrooms, drained	1
1	can (10 oz/284 mL) condensed cream of celery soup	1
1	can (10 oz/284 mL) condensed cream of Cheddar soup	1
1/3 cup	milk	75 mL
1 tsp	dried parsley flakes	5 mL

In large saucepan of water, parboil cauliflower, carrots, and sprouts until tender but crisp. Drain and place in 8-cup (2-L) casserole. Add drained mushrooms to vegetables.

In medium-size bowl, combine celery soup, Cheddar soup, milk, and parsley flakes. Pour over vegetables in casserole, stir lightly, and bake, uncovered, in 400°F (200°C) oven for 35 minutes.

Makes 6 to 8 servings.

Yorkshire Pudding

Yorkshire pudding is traditionally served with roast beef (page 54). Pat Wenger uses pan drippings when she makes this dish. Many of the leaner cuts of beef we use today do not provide enough drippings, so we often have to substitute oil.

1 cup	all-purpose flour	250 mL
¼ tsp	salt	1 mL
1 cup	cold milk	250 mL
2	eggs	2
	Canola oil or pan drippings	

TIP: The secret to a good Yorkshire pudding is a cold batter and a very hot oiled tray.

In bowl, mix together flour and salt. In separate bowl, beat eggs with milk; add flour mixture, beating until smooth. Refrigerate for 1 hour.

Using muffin tray, place ½ tsp (2 mL) canola oil or drippings in each of 12 muffin cups. Place tray into 400°F (200°C) oven for a few minutes.

Remove tray from oven and divide cold Yorkshire mixture between muffin cups. Return to 400°F (200°C) oven for 20 minutes or until puffed and golden.

Makes 12 puddings.

Desserts and Baked Goods

Apple Cake

Apple Cake generally uses buttermilk instead of shortening and the sweetness of the apples replaces some of the sugars, making this cake a lot healthier for your family. It's really "kid friendly" too.

2-1/4 cups	all-purpose flour	550 mL
1 cup	granulated sugar	250 mL
2-1/4 tsp	cinnamon	11 mL
1 tsp	baking soda	5 mL
1/4 tsp	nutmeg	1 mL
Pinch	mace	Pinch
3	eggs	3
1/2 cup	applesauce	125 mL
1/2 cup	buttermilk	125 mL
1 tsp	vanilla	5 mL
1	apple, finely chopped	1
1/2 cup	raisins	125 mL
	Brown sugar	

Sift together flour, sugar, cinnamon, baking soda, nutmeg, and mace.

In mixing bowl on low speed, mix eggs, applesauce, buttermilk, and vanilla.

Add dry ingredients to mixer in thirds, mixing on low after each addition until incorporated.

Mix in chopped apples and raisins by hand. Pour into greased and floured 10-inch (4-L) baking pan and sprinkle with brown sugar to taste. Bake in 350°F (180°C) oven for 50 minutes or until cake springs back when lightly touched. Cool in pan, then remove to rack to cool completely.

Chocolate Swirl Cheesecake

This cheesecake is a beautiful and delicious addition to any buffet.

Crust:

1-1/2 cups	chocolate wafer crumbs	375 mL
1/4 cup	melted butter	50 mL
2 tbsp	granulated sugar	25 mL

Filling:

3	pkg (each 8 oz/225 g) cream cheese	3
1 cup	granulated sugar	250 mL
3 tbsp	all-purpose flour	45 mL
2 tbsp	amaretto liqueur	25 mL
1/2 tsp	vanilla	2 mL
3	eggs	3
3 oz	semisweet chocolate, melted	75 g
2 oz	white chocolate, melted	50 g
	chocolate curls for garnish (see sidebar)	

TIP: To make chocolate curls, soften 2 oz (50 g) semisweet chocolate squares until a vegetable peeler can be run down short side of square to form curls.

CRUST:

Combine crumbs, melted butter and 2 tbsp (25 mL) sugar. Press mixture onto bottom of 9-inch (23-cm) springform pan. Bake in 325°F (160°C) for 10 minutes. Remove from oven and let cool on rack.

FILLING:

In large mixing bowl, beat cream cheese, sugar, flour, amaretto, and vanilla until smooth. Add eggs, one at a time, beating well after each addition. Pour filling over crust, reserving 1/2 cup (125 mL) of filling.

Divide reserved filling mixture, stirring half into each type of melted chocolate.

Drop by spoonfuls onto filling and swirl into pattern with knife. Bake in 425°F (220°C) oven for 10 minutes. Reduce heat to 250°F (120°C) and bake for 30 to 35 minutes or until center of cake is barely firm. Remove from oven and run knife around sides of the cake. Let cool completely before removing sides of pan. Chill until firm. Mound chocolate curls on cake.

Apple Crisp

TIP: For a change of flavor, add ⅓ cup (75 mL) raisins or fresh or frozen cranberries to the apple slices.

TIP: There are many variations to this recipe. Instead of apples, you can substitute peaches, pears, prune plums, or a berry mixture.

This version of an old standby is from Lisa Richards. It's doubly delicious served with whipped cream or ice cream.

4 cups	peeled and sliced apples	1 L
¾ cup	granulated sugar	175 mL
1-¼ cups	all-purpose flour	300 mL
½ tsp	cinnamon	2 mL
¾ cup	brown sugar	175 mL
½ cup	rolled oats	125 mL
½ cup	butter	125 mL

In bowl, combine apples, granulated sugar, ¼ cup (50 mL) flour, and cinnamon. Place in 8-inch (2-L) square baking dish.

Stir together remaining 1 cup (250 mL) flour, brown sugar, and rolled oats. Cut butter into dry ingredients and crumble over apple mixture in baking dish. Bake in 375°F (190°C) oven for 35 minutes or until apples are fork-tender and topping browned.

Makes 4 to 6 servings.

Bachelor's No-Bake Pie

This recipe comes from a very dear friend, Jan Johnston, of Zepherhills, Florida. It's so easy, even a "bachelor" can make it—hence the name. This version is low fat too.

1	can (12 oz/340 mL) crushed pineapple, drained	1
2 cups	low-fat sour cream	500 mL
1	pkg (4 oz/113 g) sugar-free instant vanilla pudding mix	1
1	10-inch (25-cm) graham cracker pie crust	1
	Low-fat whipped dessert topping	

In large bowl, mix pineapple, sour cream, and instant pudding mix. Beat well until thoroughly mixed and pour into graham cracker crust.

Top with low-fat whipped dessert topping; chill and enjoy.

Makes 6 to 8 servings.

Best-Ever Pastry

TIP: If you need a quick pastry and want to use a mix, try Robin Hood Pastry Mix.

Pat Wenger makes the best pastry (and pies) in town. Pat is the most energetic lady I've ever met. Gems has been fortunate to have Pat on its volunteer team for the past four years. She constantly and unselfishly gives of herself to family and friends.

5 cups	all-purpose flour	1.25 L
1 tsp	baking powder	5 mL
1/2 tsp	salt	2 mL
1 lb	Tenderflake lard	500 g
1	egg	1
	Milk	

In bowl, combine four, baking powder, and salt. Cut in lard with pastry blender (or rub in with fingertips) until mixture looks like cornmeal. In 1-cup (250-mL) measuring cup, mix egg and enough milk to make 1 full cup (250 mL).

Add egg mixture to flour mixture and stir with fork, adding only enough milk to make dough hold together. Gather dough into ball and divide into 6 portions. (Each portion makes a single pie crust.) Wrap and refrigerate unused portions.

Roll out portion to be used on lightly floured surface (if dough is sticking, chill for 1 to 2 hours).

Makes enough for 6 pie shells or 3 double-crust pies.

Better than Brownies

The calories don't count if you eat these standing up! At least that's what Bev Love says and she makes these all the time.

2 oz	unsweetened chocolate	50 g
½ cup	shortening	125 mL
1 cup	granulated sugar	250 mL
3	eggs	3
1 tsp	vanilla	5 mL
¾ cup	sifted all-purpose flour	175 mL
1 tsp	baking powder	5 mL
½ tsp	salt	2 mL
1 cup	chopped nuts (optional)	250 mL

In bowl over hot water, melt chocolate. Cool bowl slightly, then beat in sugar. Add eggs one at a time, beating well after each addition; stir in vanilla.

In separate bowl, sift together flour, baking powder, and salt; stir into chocolate mixture, then stir in nuts (if using).

Pour into greased 8-inch (2-L) square pan. Bake in 325°F (160°C) oven for 30 minutes. Cool; top with chocolate frosting or sifted icing sugar if you like.

Makes about 16 squares.

Carrot Cake

This is a very moist cake and an all-time favorite. You can sprinkle icing sugar (through a sieve) over the cooled cake or use the decadent Cream Cheese Icing that follows.

4	eggs	4
2 cups	granulated sugar	500 mL
1 cup	vegetable oil	250 mL
2-1/2 cups	all-purpose flour	625 mL
2 tsp	baking soda	10 mL
2 tsp	cinnamon	10 mL
1 tsp	baking powder	5 mL
1 tsp	salt	5 mL
1/2 cup	raisins	125 mL
4 cups	grated raw carrots (about 1 lb/500 g)	1 L
	Cream Cheese Icing (recipe follows)	

In large bowl, beat together eggs and sugar until fluffy; beat in oil.

In separate bowl, combine flour, baking soda, cinnamon, baking powder, and salt. Stir into egg mixture. Stir in raisins and carrots.

Pour into greased 9-inch (2.5-L) springform pan lined with waxed paper. Bake in 350°F (180°C) oven for 1 hour or until toothpick inserted in center comes out clean. Remove rim of pan and cool completely. Remove waxed paper and bottom of pan.

When cool, if frosting, split cake into two layers and ice first layer; set second layer on top and cover cake with icing.

Cream Cheese Icing:

8 oz	cream cheese, at room temperature	225 g
1/2 cup	butter, at room temperature	125 mL
1 tsp	vanilla	5 mL
3 cups	icing sugar	750 mL

In large bowl, beat together cream cheese, butter, and vanilla. Gradually beat in icing sugar to give smooth spreadable consistency. Makes enough to frost layer cakes.

Cherries Jubilee

Here's a very dramatic dessert, fit for a king or queen.

1 tbsp	cornstarch	15 mL
1 tbsp	granulated sugar	15 mL
1	can (12 oz/341 mL) pitted black cherries	1
3 to 4	strips orange zest	3 to 4
1 tsp	lemon juice	5 mL
½ cup	warm brandy	125 mL
6	large scoops vanilla ice cream	6

In saucepan, mix cornstarch and sugar together; add liquid from canned cherries (about 1 cup/250 mL) and orange zest; stir. Cook until sauce thickens; discard orange zest and add cherries and lemon juice.

When serving, have cherry mixture warm in chafing dish and large ice cream scoops in shallow bowl.

To serve, pour brandy over cherry mixture and flame by touching match to mixture. Place ice cream scoop on glass dish and top with cherry mixture.

Makes 6 servings.

Chocolate Apple Cake

Chocolate and apple are a simple yet sublime combination.

1-1/2 cups	all-purpose flour	375 mL
1/2 cup	unsweetened cocoa powder	125 mL
1-1/2 tsp	baking powder	7 mL
1/2 tsp	each baking soda and salt	2 mL
1-1/4 cups	granulated sugar	300 mL
1/2 cup	butter, melted	125 mL
1/2 cup	buttermilk	125 mL
2	eggs	2
1 tbsp	vanilla	15 mL
2 cups	peeled and coarsely chopped tart apples	500 mL
1/2 cup	semisweet chocolate chips	125 mL

TIP: This is a moist cake and doesn't need icing. When cool, sift a little icing sugar over the top and serve.

In large bowl, sift together flour, cocoa, baking powder, baking soda, and salt.

In another bowl, combine sugar, butter, and buttermilk until well blended. Stir in eggs and vanilla. Pour mixture over dry ingredients and thoroughly combine.

Stir in apples and chocolate chips. Pour into greased and floured 13- x 9-inch (3.5-L) baking pan. Bake in 350°F (180°C) oven for 30 to 40 minutes or until tester inserted in center comes out clean.

Chocolate-Dipped Strawberries

TIP: **You can use other fruits when strawberries are not in season— orange sections are particularly good. Hold orange section on a toothpick to dip into chocolate.**

Debbie Farquhar suggested this simple dessert as a very elegant way to finish a summer meal.

1 cup	semisweet chocolate chips	250 mL
1 tbsp	shortening	15 mL
	Strawberries, washed	

In the top of double boiler, melt chocolate and shortening until smooth. Holding stem, dip strawberries, one at a time, into chocolate. Place on waxed paper to set. Chill and serve.

Chocolate Trifle

This amazing (but easy) dessert was sent to us by Lisa Richards. Lisa loves to cook and entertain. She is a quality assurance manager at Etrade Canada.

1	chocolate cake mix	1
3	large pkg chocolate pudding and pie filling	3
6 cups	milk	1.5 L
2	large pkg whipped dessert topping mix	2
4	bars Crispy Crunch or Skor	4
1/2 cup	Bailey's Irish Cream	125 mL

Bake cake according to package directions and let cool (use 2 round layer cake pans). Prepare puddings using milk. Whip dessert topping, if not using pre-whipped brand; crumble chocolate bars.

To assemble: In large serving bowl, crumble 1 cake layer. Sprinkle half of Irish Cream on top of cake; spread half pudding on top of cake and Irish Cream. Spread half of dessert topping on pudding layer. Sprinkle chocolate bar pieces over dessert topping. Repeat process starting with second cake layer. Chill several hours and serve.

Makes about 8 to 10 servings.

Crunchy Baked Bananas

Here's another dessert fit for kids. Let them make it themselves—under your supervision of course.

2 or 3	large bananas	2 or 3
2 tbsp	brown sugar	25 mL
½ cup	miniature marshmallows	125 mL
½ cup	cornflakes	125 mL
1 tbsp	melted butter	15 mL

Peel bananas and cut lengthwise; arrange in buttered baking dish.

Sprinkle brown sugar on bananas; cover with marshmallows.

Mix together cornflakes and melted butter; sprinkle on top. Bake in 375°F (190°C) oven for 12 to 15 minutes or until marshmallows have melted.

Makes 4 servings.

Easy Maple Fudge

Lisa Richards makes this delectable fudge and sent in the recipe.

2 cups	brown sugar	500 mL
½ cup	butter	125 mL
½ cup	cream or canned evaporated milk	125 mL
½ cup	cake-and-pastry flour	125 mL
1 tsp	vanilla	5 mL

TIP: You can substitute ½ cup (125 mL) all-purpose flour and 4 tsp (20 mL) cornstarch for the cake-and-pastry flour.

In saucepan, mix sugar, butter, and cream and boil for 8 minutes. Add flour and vanilla; beat until creamy.

Turn mixture into buttered 8-inch (2-L) square pan. Score into squares while warm; cut when cool and firm.

Makes 16 two-inch (5-cm) squares.

Belle Lancaster's Gingerbread

TIP: To sour and
enrich the milk, pour
about 3 to 4 tbsp
(45 to 60 mL) of sour
cream into measur-
ing cup and fill cup
to desired measure
with milk. Whisk
with a fork.

*Stevie Cameron, investigative journalist and author, said this recipe has been
made in her family for generations. Belle Lancaster, who was a wonderful cook,
worked for Stevie's grandmother, Tassie, and used to made this scrumptious cake
for everyone. "My grandmother said she could always tell a bad cookbook by
checking its gingerbread recipe—if it calls for hot water instead of sour cream,
don't buy it!"*

1 cup	brown sugar	250 mL
1/2 cup	table molasses (not blackstrap)	125 mL
4 tbsp	melted butter	60 mL
1	egg (2, if eggs are small)	1
2 tsp	baking powder	10 mL
	(if sour milk is used, use to 1/2 tsp/2 mL	
	baking soda and 1 tsp/5 mL	
	baking powder instead)	
2 to 3 tsp	ground ginger	10 to 15 mL
1/2 tsp	each ground cinnamon,	2 mL
	ground nutmeg, and salt	
2 cups	sifted all-purpose flour	500 mL
3/4 cup	milk (preferably soured with cream)	175 mL

Grease and flour a 9-inch (2.5-L) square baking pan.

Cream together sugar, molasses, melted butter, and eggs. (May be
done in mixer.) Set aside. In a large bowl, stir baking soda/baking
powder, ginger, cinnamon, nutmeg, and salt into flour. Stir half of the
milk into the sugar-molasses-egg mixture. Stir in half flour mixture until
everything is just blended. (This can be done in mixer on low speed.)
Stir in remaining milk and then remaining flour mixture. Do not stir too
much—just until everything is well blended. Pour into the prepared
baking pan and bake in 325°F (160°C) oven for about 35 to 40 minutes,

or until gingerbread has risen and is starting to pull away from sides of pan. (A larger recipe may take an extra 10 minutes or so; test with toothpick.) It should be rich and still very moist. It may even fall a bit when you take it out. Cut in pan while still warm if possible.

Makes 9 servings.

Fried Bananas

This is one of the world's easiest and best desserts. Flaming the bananas in the brandy will burn off the alcohol but leave a wonderful flavor.

½ cup	butter	125 mL
½ cup	brown sugar	125 mL
4	bananas	4
¼ cup	brandy or rum	50 mL

In large skillet over medium-high heat, melt butter; add brown sugar. Slice bananas in half, lengthwise, and fry in butter-sugar mixture.

Heat brandy or rum; pour over bananas and flame. Serve with vanilla ice cream.

Makes 4 servings.

Sinfully Chocolate Cake

Here's an absolute must *for any chocolate lover.*

2 cups	semisweet chocolate chips	500 mL
1 tbsp	hot water	15 mL
4	egg yolks, beaten	4
¼ to ½ cup	melted butter	50 to 125 mL
1-½ tsp	granulated sugar	7 mL
1-½ cups	all-purpose flour	375 mL
4	egg whites, stiffly beaten	4
	Whipped cream	
	Chocolate shavings or curls	
	(sidebar page 111)	

In saucepan over medium-low heat, melt chocolate chips with hot water. Stir in beaten egg yolks, melted butter, and sugar. Stir in flour.

Fold some of beaten egg whites into chocolate mixture, then pour all of chocolate mixture into remaining egg whites and gently fold until fully incorporated.

Pour batter into greased 10-inch (3-L) springform pan lined with waxed paper and bake in 350°F (180°C) oven for 30 minutes or until tester inserted in center of cake comes out clean.

Let cool for 3 minutes before removing from pan. Serve slices warm, garnished with whipped cream and chocolate shavings.

Index

curry
    Dal, 47
    lentil, 47
    orange curried rice, 101
    potato and cauliflower, 53

D

Dal curry, 47
desserts
    see also baked goods
    bananas, crunchy baked, 122
    bananas, fried, 126
    cakes. *See* cakes
    cherries jubilee, 118
    chocolate swirl cheesecake,
        111
    chocolate trifle, 121
    fudge, maple, 123
    no-bake pie, 113
    pastry, 113
    strawberries, chocolate-
        dipped, 120
dips
    crab dip, hot, 18
    guacamole, 19

E

eggs
    and potato cake, 48
    seafood omelette, 93

F

Farquhar, Debbie, 41, 64,
    99, 120
Fernandes, Olinda, 47, 53
Festival of Hope, 37
fettuccine
    Alfredo, 49
    with scallops in cream and
        garlic sauce, 91

fish
    haddock, baked, 86
    salmon, grilled steaks, 87
    salmon, oven-poached, 89
    salmon chowder, 32
    sole amandine, 94
fried bananas, 126
fruits
    apple cake, 110
    apple chocolate cake, 119
    apple crisp, 112
    bananas, baked, 122
    bananas, fried, 126
    cherries jubilee, 118
    peach chutney, 102
    strawberries, chocolate-
        dipped, 120
fudge, maple, 123

G

garlic soup, 28
gazpacho, chunky, 29
Gems of Hope, about, 9–11
Gibson, Leanne, 35
gingerbread, 124–125
Global Education Medical
    Supplies (GEMS) Inc., 9
gorgonzola
    dressing, 40
    sauce, 76
Grassroots College project, 10
Greek salad, 39
grilled vegetables, 99
ground beef
    beef and pasta bake, 55
    chili con carne, 61
    meatballs, in vermouth, 25–26
    meatballs, sweet and sour, 22
    shepherd's pie, 56
    Tam Tam, 58
guacamole, 19

H

haddock, baked, 86
ham and cheese strata, 66
hearts of palm, 13
herb-spice rub, 57
hollandaise sauce, 72–73

I

icing, cream cheese, 117

J

Johnston, Jan, 113

L

lamb
    braised shanks, 64
    chops, with pasta and garlic
        hollandaise, 63
    grilled leg of, 62
Lancaster, Belle, 124
lasagna, meatless, 52
legumes. *See* beans and legumes
lentils
    Dal curry, 47
    soup, spicy, 33
lime sauce, 90
lobster, seafood Newburg, 92
Luke, Melissa, 97, 98

M

macaroni vegetable medley with
    wine, 51
main courses. *See* meatless main
    courses; meats; poultry
maple fudge, 123
meatballs, in vermouth, 25–26
meatballs, sweet and sour, 22
meatless main courses
    black bean and corn chili, 44
    egg and potato cake, 48
    fettuccine Alfredo, 49

    lasagna, meatless, 52
    macaroni vegetable medley
      with wine, 51
    mushroom, broccoli and
        rice bake, 46
    pasta with summer vegetables,
      50
    peppers, cottage cheese-
        stuffed, 45
    potato and cauliflower curry,
      53
meats
    beef and pasta bake, 55
    beef bourguignon, 59
    beef brochettes, 60
    chili con carne, 61
    ham and cheese strata, 66
    lamb, braised shanks, 64
    lamb, grilled leg of, 62
    lamb chops, with pasta and
      garlic hollandaise, 63
    meatballs, in vermouth, 25–26
    meatballs, sweet and sour, 22
    pork and peppers, 67
    pork roast, glazed, 65
    rib roast of beef, standing, 54
    sausage and potatoes,
      country style, 70
    sausage quiche, crustless, 68
    shepherd's pie, 56
    spareribs, oven-barbecued, 69
    steak with herb-spice rub, 57
    Tam Tam, 58
    tortière, 71
    veal, screwdriver (with vodka),
      74
    veal Oscar, 72
    veal parmesan, 75
    veal scallops, with gorgonzola
      sauce, 76
minestrone, 30

Dear Reader,

In case you haven't heard about us, GEMS OF HOPE is a charity that works with women and helps them to help themselves. Unlike many charities, *we help women to become independent*, and to support themselves through very small (micro) business development.

We fund local partner organizations like ourselves, who then make loans available for small business to groups of women and men, who are responsible as groups for the repayment. These small groups are called "village banks" and they are key to sustainable development, since they quickly become independent of outside aid. We complement our micro-enterprise loans with community health and education programs to make sure that the chances of success are optimized.

This cookbook, besides being a valuable collection of recipes, is a way for us to support our programs. Every dollar we raise by sale of the book brings us a match of another dollar by the Canadian International Development Agency (CIDA). The money goes a long way in the Global South to help women gain more control over their lives, their home economy, and their role in society.

Thank you for your help. Your money is going to a good cause, and we know you will enjoy the recipes!!

John Paterson
Executive Director

P.S. If you would like more information about GEMS OF HOPE, please contact the office at 675 King Street West, Suite 305, Toronto, Ontario, M5V 1M9. We can be reached by phone at (416) 362-4367, or by fax at (416) 362-4170.